Magic Pillows, Hidden Quilts!

Karin Hellaby

Preceding pages: Through the Portholes *by Karin Hellaby (front cover);* Razzle Dazzle *by Teresa Wardlaw (p.1);* Stars in the Cabin *by Heather Langdon (p.3). Back cover, left to right:* Go Go Gecko *by Pat Matthes;* Cobwebs in the Windows *by Shirley Hughes;* Desert Jewels *by Pippa Moss.*

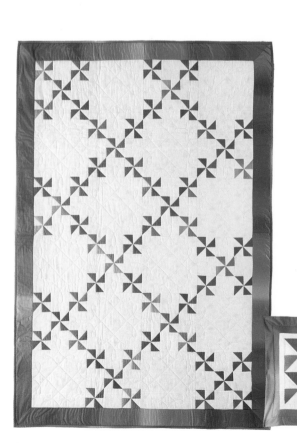

On this page: Celtic Stars *(top left) by Susan Prior;* Rainbow Pinwheels *(left) by Janet Last;* Summer Skies *(top right) by John Hazon; and* Oriental Treasures *(above) by Jan Allen.*

Magic Pillows, Hidden Quilts!

Hellaby

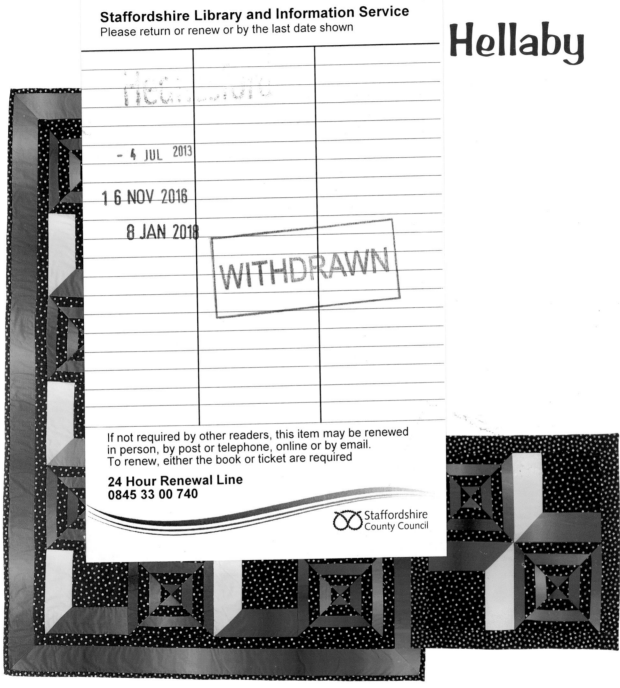

Quilters Haven
Publications

Acknowledgements

This book is for Jason, my second son, aged seventeen.

His input into this book, with computer knowledge, design choices and much encouragement, has been invaluable. I hope the support he has given me will be repaid by the financial support I can give him as he approaches higher education.

Many local quilters tested the instructions and patterns in this book and I am very grateful for their help, suggestions and critique.

Fabric was provided by Timeless Treasures UK and Oakcraft, two UK distributors who gave the testers free choice from their wonderful samples.

Rosemary, Allan and Colin have again proved invaluable in making the manuscript into a book, and second time round it all seemed easier! (Or was that my imagination?)

I really appreciate having a graphic artist who has many years of quilting knowledge, and Rosemary's suggestions have helped to develop the original concept of this book.

I am lucky to have a seemingly endless supply of students and customers who are willing to proof read and check at a moments notice.

To all who helped with this book a big 'thank you'.

First published by
Quilters Haven Publications in 2002

Copyright © Karin Hellaby 2002

Graphics by Rosemary Muntus

Layout by Allan Scott

Photography by Neil Porter, The Field House, John Carr's Terrace, Clifton, Bristol BS8 1DW

Printed by EAM Printers, Ipswich, Suffolk

ISBN 0-9540928-1-3   UPC 7-44674-06020-4

Quilters Haven Publications
68 High Street, Wickham Market
Suffolk, UK
IP13 0QU

Tel: +44 (0)1728 746275 Fax: +44 (0)1394 610525

www.quilters-haven.co.uk

Chapter guide

Introduction

What fun! How useful! How impressive! Do that again! Can you make me one?

These are some of the many comments I have heard when I show people a 'quillow' – a particular kind of magic pillow.

What looks like a cushion or a pillow opens out to form a lap-size quilt – and when you have finished using it, you can fold the quilt back into the 'pillow', which is really a pocket firmly attached to the quilt!

I first came across a Magic Pillow twelve years ago, when I started teaching patchwork and quiltmaking. One of my students had a Canadian visitor who always took a quillow with her when she travelled. We examined this "new' quilt with considerable interest, and inevitably I was asked to teach a class: everyone wanted to know how a quillow was made. So I worked out a method of making them – and I have been teaching it ever since.

The lap and mini quilts in this book are based on fun patchwork patterns that are machine pieced and 'grow' quickly. Because these quilts spend a lot of their time folded up and out of sight, I don't usually feel the inclination to sew elaborate patchwork that needs to be admired. In fact these are the quilts I can give away without worrying about how they are used – after all, I have not spent a long time making them. So I never worried if my own children used their quillows as dressing gowns in the morning while they were eating breakfast – or found them useful as capes when they were playing Batman and Robin. And they were great on long car journeys, or to wrap up a sick child who wanted to be on the sofa in front of the TV.

Another magic pillow evolved separately (not as a quillow) as I made quilted patchwork pillow slips that could hide a folded quilt. This has become a neat way to store a quilt which is magically there just when you need it.

Finally, I have included a simple quilted square with corner ties. This wraps around a quilt to make a pillow, with the ties holding everything in place. Another magic pillow!

However, there is a warning that comes with this book: 'Magic pillows are addictive, and you will never be allowed to make just one.'

With the techniques in this book, that won't be a problem!

Using this book

First choose a pattern or a combination of patterns for your quilt top. Then decide on the size – either a lap quilt or a mini quilt, and make the patchwork top, adding borders. If you are making a quillow – make the patchwork pillow front.

Assemble into a quillow, lap or mini quilt.

Further option – make a separate pillow to hide or to store the quilt.

The quilt patterns are designed so that they all finish as a patchwork top measuring 36" x 54".They are composed of blocks that are 9" square (finished size). The patterns can be worked quickly, some in a day!

The Lap Quilt (44" x 62")

The lap quilt has been designed to include 24 blocks (4 x 6). As all the patchwork blocks measure 9" they are interchangeable so that you can combine them into quilts that you have designed yourself, or use one of the lovely combinations we have created.

The borders (4" wide) are added to enclose the patchwork, and bring the quilt top to a finished size of approximately 44" x 62". The 44" width measurement is similar to the width of the 100% cottons available in a quilt shop. This means that the quilt backing can be a length of 62", and requires no piecing.

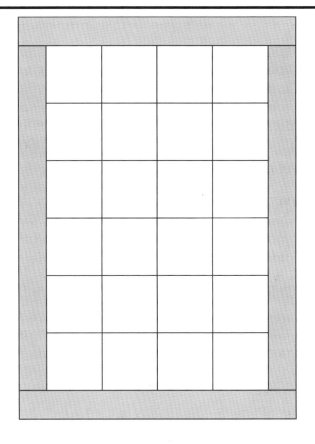

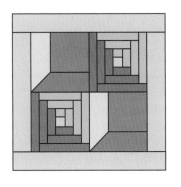

Grid for the lap quilt (right), the pillow front (left) and a quillow design (below, right) using Log Cabin and Attic Window blocks

For the pillow front you can use a patchwork design that is similar to the quilt top, or choose something different from the many block patterns in the book. Four blocks are used for the pillow, and then a border is added to make it large enough for a quilt to fit comfortably inside.

You will find details of two different assembly methods for quillows; just choose the one that suits you best.

Alternatively you may choose to make a lap quilt, or a fleece-backed throw, without the pillow. You can make an attractive separate pillow to hide the quilt when it is not in use.

Finally, to quickly finish your quilt, tie with a variety of utilitarian quilting stitches.

The Mini Quilt (33" x 42")

This is ideal for giving to a baby or toddler: it's perfect for little ones because it is only half the size of the lap quilt.

You could also use this size as a wall hanging or as a crib quilt.

Use the 9" blocks in any combination, but remember that this time you only need to make twelve blocks for the quilt top and one extra for the quillow.

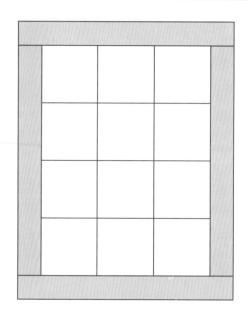

The fabric needed for the mini-quilt is half that required for the lap quilt.

The finished size of the quilt will be 33" x 42", including a 3" border all round.

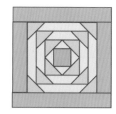

The pillow itself is made from one 9" block, with a border added to bring it up to the required size.

Magic pillows

There is more than one way to make a magic pillow – and in this book you will find three of them.

The **quillow cushion** becomes a part of the quilt itself, and the quilt is folded away inside it when not in use.

The **slip-in pillow** allows you to separate the quilt from the pillow if you wish.

The **wrap-around pillow** derives from Japanese concepts of paper and fabric wrapping; it is an elegant way of creating another, rather different look for your magic pillow.

The example quilts – and the project pages – show all three types of pillow and how to make them. For your project, choose the one that best suits your own ideas.

What do I need?

Equipment

Sewing machine: the quick construction methods used in this book require a simple straight stitch sewing machine. I find a ¼" seam foot essential. If one is not available for your machine, mark the bed of the sewing machine with masking tape, or buy an 'angler tool' to give you the necessary guidelines. A walking foot attachment is a help when assembling and machine quilting; it stops the layers from shifting.

Rotary cutting set: i.e. a mat, ruler and cutter. The instructions in this book have been written for rotary cutting, because it is a faster and more accurate method of cutting fabric than using scissors. I use an Omnigrid mat and ruler set as I know the measurements are accurate, easy to see and match each other. A 9½" Omnigrid square is useful: it corresponds to the block size.

Invisigrip: a clear, non-slip film that prevents rulers from slipping when you are rotary cutting. You can still slide the ruler into position; but when you are cutting, the pressure of your hand on the ruler stops any movement.

Scissors: a small pair for cutting and snipping threads, a larger pair for cutting fabric. I like the Clover range and use their patchwork scissors which have a serrated edge which helps to 'hold' the fabric and small cutwork scissors that have a leather sheath to protect the blades. The Gingher range of scissors are also good. Always choose scissors that cut to the point.

Iron: consider using a travel iron, as it is lighter and has no steam holes which can catch the fabric. Many prefer a heavy iron as it 'presses' better. Keep a water spray bottle close by to help with stubborn creases. Steam is rarely required in patchwork, and can distort your work.

Thread: use cotton thread when sewing together cotton fabric. For quilting and tying it is best to use the specialist threads that are available.

Pins: flower head pins are 2" long, fine and very sharp: ideal for pinning seams together when machine stitching. The flower heads lie flat so that a ruler can be placed on top without distortion.

Safety pins: I use 1" solid brass gilt safety pins which do not rust and have sharp polished points for fastening the quilt layers before quilting. If you suffer from arthritis try the curved safety pins, as they are easier to insert and close.

Machine needles: need to be replaced after 6–8 hours of sewing! Size 70/10 or 80/12.

Hand sewing needles: sew with good quality needles that you feel comfortable using. For utility tying/quilting use needles with larger eyes to thread the thicker yarn, e.g. embroidery or doll's needles.

Marking tools

Mechanical propelling pencil

Chaco-liner: used to draw fine temporary chalk lines. The unit contains powdered chalk which is released when the wheel at the base rotates. Available in blue, pink, yellow and white.

Fabric

All the fabrics used in this book are 100% cotton quilting fabrics. Quilt shops selling this book have details of the fabrics used in the projects, and can order them or suggest suitable alternatives. The expert staff in your local quilt shop can help you choose fabrics from their wonderful selections.

Most projects need only three or four fabrics. Instead of choosing just one fabric in a particular colour, try selecting smaller quantities of several fabrics that all read the same colour: why choose one blue when six blues can look more exciting? Quilters all have one thing in common: they love fabrics, and need no excuse to add as many as they can to one quilt.

In order to see the patchwork design you need contrast between the fabrics. This can be a light value contrast or a colour contrast. It is this contrast that emphasises different parts of the design and is an important factor when making your choice.

Wadding/batting

There are many different waddings available and each quilter has their favourites. I recommend the following types for different projects in the book.

Pillows: low loft such as a 100% needle punched cotton, which has the advantage that you can iron it, and cottons 'stick' to one another. Or use a good quality low loft polyester.

Lap Quillow quilt: because the quilt flattens in time from being squashed inside a pillow I prefer to a use medium to high loft when machine stitching or tying. If you are hand quilting, check that the wadding is suitable for this purpose.

Mini quillow: low loft polyester. If this is a gift for a child, choose a cotton or wool wadding rather than polyester.

Mini-quilt used as a wall hanging: choose a wadding that will hang well without curling. The firm, needled waddings in cotton and polyester are very suitable.

In the UK low loft is known as a 2oz and high loft as a 4oz wadding.

Polar fleece

Polar fleece is now a firm favourite with my students, and several of the quilts in this book are backed with fleece.

Using fleece as a backing eliminates the need for the middle layer of wadding, which technically make these projects not quilts but 'throws'. The result is very cuddly, and it looks and feels great.

When layering with the quilt top, ensure that the fleece is not stretched. Safety pins are best for temporarily holding the two layers together.

I recommend using utility hand quilting or machine quilting to attach the patchwork top to the fleece permanently . The layers are too thick for fine hand quilting.

I always use a fabric binding on quilts that have fleece as a backing to give a neat edge and good finish.

Washing fabrics before use

Some quilters never pre-wash fabric others always do. The decision is yours!

There may be excess dye in fabric and you may be concerned about shrinkage – all good reasons for pre-washing fabric. I prefer to hand wash fabric in separate colour groups so that I can actually see if there is dye loss. Use the best quality gentlest detergent. Rinse well. Dry in the dryer or out of direct sunlight and iron whilst still damp. At this stage I often spray starch and iron as I find the fabric easier to rotary cut accurately if it has some stiffness.

If there is dye loss after rinsing, add a solution of one part white vinegar to two parts water as a final rinse. Alternatively you can use 'Retayne' solution to seal the dye.

Follow the manufacturers instructions for wadding or batting when making a decision on pre-washing. Most of the time it is unnecessary: certainly polar fleece requires no pre-washing.

Fabric shopping list

These yardages are for fabric that is a minimum 43″ wide.

Quilt Top

Choose your pattern – you will need to decide on lap size or mini size.

The pattern fabric quantities are for lap size quilts. If you are choosing a mini quilt, then halve the fabric quantities. The figures do allow for a few mistakes!

Quilt Border

| Lap size | 1 yard |
| Mini size | ½ yard |

Usually the border fabric is one that already appears in the quilt. You may wish to make your choice once the patchwork centre is complete. But will your quilt shop still have the fabric?

Quilt Backing

| Lap size | 1¾ yards |
| Mini size | 1 yard |

Binding (if required)

| Lap size | ¾ yard |
| Mini size | ½ yard |

Cushion front

This can be made from the fabric that is left over from your quilt top.

Cushion back

| Lap size | ¾ yard |
| Mini size | ½ yard |

Buying in metres?

A metre is 10% more than a yard, so if you are buying in metres you can buy 10% less fabric than stated in the patterns. I suspect that most quilters prefer to keep to the same figures and put the extra fabric into their stash!

How to rotary cut

Rotary cutting has revolutionised patchwork as we can cut layers of fabric into strips and shapes without marking the fabric. This is quick and accurate. The rotary cutting set is made up of a mat, ruler and cutter. The cutter is a circular blade – very effective, and dangerous if not used correctly. Practice cutting paper instead of fabric until you feel confident. Confidence with rotary cutting only requires practice.

To cut strips of fabric

1 Iron the fabric along the warp and weft threads. Avoid ironing diagonally, as you may stretch the fabric on the bias. Fold fabric in half, selvedges together, with a good, strong crease along the fold. If you have no selvedges, iron with the fold along the straight of the grain.

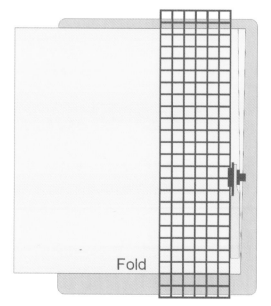

Fold

2 Place fabric on unmarked side of rotary cutting mat, folded edge nearest you. Lay ruler on top, matching a horizontal line of the ruler to the fabric fold. Use your left hand to hold the ruler in place – if the ruler moves, consider using Invisigrip.

3 Rotary cut against the right side of the ruler (left handers rotary cut on the left). Remove safety cover on the cutter and lean the cutter against the ruler; hold it firmly, pushing it down with your index finger. Start cutting before crossing the bottom fold, pushing away from you. Always cut away from you, and when you complete the cut, **replace the safety guard.** This first cut straightens the edge of the fabric.

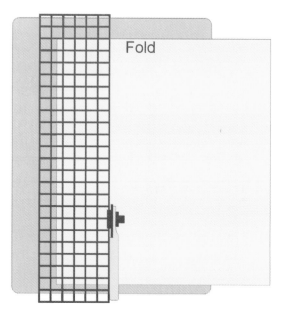

Fold

4 Turn the mat through 180°, or walk to the opposite side of the board. The straight edge you have cut will now be on your left.

5 You are now ready to cut fabric strips. Place the ruler so the exact width measurement you need is precisely aligned to the newly cut edge of the fabric, ensuring the fold is still lined up with one of the horizontal guidelines. Rotary cut as before.

QH Tip

If you are left-handed, check these diagrams in a mirror to see how you need to work with the cutter.

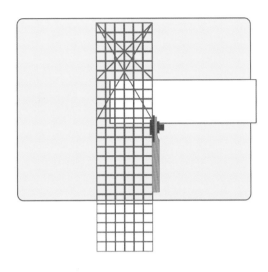

Multiple squares from strips

Using 4½″ squares as an example:

1 Place a pre-cut 4½″ fabric strip on the mat. This will be cut while still folded.

2 Square up the strip selvedge end, removing the selvedge completely.

3 Turn the mat through 180°.

4 Lay the ruler on the fabric so that the 4½″ mark lines up with the newly cut edge, and the top of the fabric is in line with a ruler line. Rotary cut. Each cut will give you two squares.

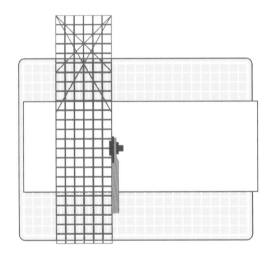

For strips and squares larger than the width of your ruler:

1 Use the printed side of the mat; line up the cut edge of the fabric against the 0 line down the side of the mat.

2 Position the strip so that it runs along the parallel lines of the mat; place the ruler on the correct vertical line and cut.

Cutting one square

Using a 9″ square as an example:

1 Place the 9½″ square ruler in the bottom left-hand corner of the fabric. Trim away excess fabric on the right and top edges.

2 Remove the ruler, and rotate the fabric square through 180°.

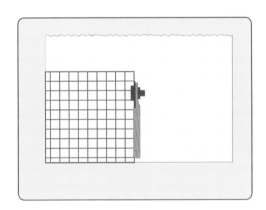

3 Place the 9″ lines of the ruler on the newly cut edges.

4 Cut the remaining two sides of your square to the right and along the top of the repositioned ruler.

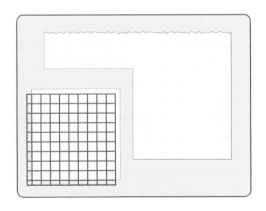

Hints and tips

- Unless you are told otherwise, always sew your **seams** with a scant ¼" seam allowance. (i.e one or two threads less than ¼"). This is more accurate than an exact ¼" because there is a small amount of fabric lost due to the thickness of the thread and the bulk created by pressing the seam allowances in one direction.

- **Sew straight seams** with a slightly smaller than medium stitch, no tying off is needed unless indicated. The stitching should be small enough not to come undone but large enough to 'unpick' if you go wrong.

- **To hold small pieces of fabric** when marking lines, use fine sand paper. This will help prevent the fabric from moving and the line becoming distorted.

- **Starching** the fabric before rotary cutting is a good idea as it is less likely to move.

- When **cutting same size strips** from several fabrics it is quicker and more accurate to layer the fabrics. Iron together to help them adhere to one another. Then cut multiple strips in one go. Keep the strips in layers for cutting squares and other patchwork units.

- Use a **neutral colour thread** (cream, beige, or grey) so you don't need to change thread colour when you change fabrics.

- **Sew from cut edge to cut edge**. If your machine does not like doing this, then start sewing on a folded scrap of fabric, and sew into the adjacent patchwork. Finish sewing on to a second adjacent fabric scrap. This 'thread saver' will save thread and help prevent the first and last stitches snagging.

Chain piecing speeds up sewing. Feed the patchwork pieces through the sewing machine without cutting the threads between them. Your pieces will look as if they are a line of washing. When you have finished, cut apart, snipping through the chained thread joining the pieces.

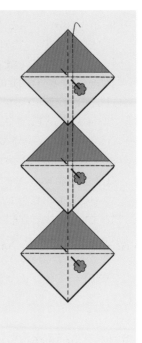

- **Pin at right angles to the seams**; that way the seams don't move and it's easy to slip the pins out as you stitch towards them. I use fine flower pins.

- When **matching two pieces of patchwork**, I pin the seams at each end and then evenly along the length. If one piece is slightly longer, pin the fabric first (matching each end) and sew with the baggy side down. Miraculously the extra fabric seems to disappear!

- **If you miss when matching points**, just unpick a few stitches either side. Re-align and then stitch. Don't attempt this more than twice as you stress the fabric and the problem gets worse. Remember not everyone is perfect!

- **Use a flower pin or stiletto to guide the fabric towards the needle**. Using the tip of your finger can be dangerous as it could disappear under the needle.

- A **'needle-stop down' position** is a great asset. If your machine has one, do use it.

When **sewing small pieces of patchwork**, pins are unnecessary; use the abutting seam technique to get perfect seam matching. Lay the pieces right sides together with seams pressed in opposite directions so that they fit together. With the top seam opposing the sewing direction, the two seams will 'nestle and wrestle' for a perfect match. I often twist the seams round to make the top seam oppose; a twisted seam inside the quilt usually goes unnoticed whereas an unmatched seam does not!

- **Fit a new machine needle** every 6–8 hours of sewing. A blunt needle damages the fabric and causes uneven stitching.

- Many people confuse **ironing and pressing**. Ironing is a back and forth sweeping motion that is used on clothes and fabrics to remove wrinkles. In quiltmaking we mostly press, which is the gentle lowering, pressing and lifting of the iron along seams. Perfectly cut and sewn patchwork can become distorted by excessive ironing.

- **Setting seam stitches**. This is a technique I frequently use as it helps to bed the stitches into the fabric. After sewing a seam I press the seam and then open up the patch and gently press it in one direction towards the darker fabric. If this is too bulky then press the seam open. Often I 'finger' press with a little wooden iron as there is less distortion. Do check that the seam is correct before you set it!

- When **sewing nine patch blocks** made from nine units, make up all the units first, sew into three separate horizontal rows, and finally sew the rows together, wrestling and nestling the seams. Use the same method when sewing blocks together into the quilt top.

- When a square is referred to as **a 9" block**, this is the finished size (i.e. its size when it is sewn in place). Its unfinished size is 9½", as there is a ¼" seam allowance around the block.

- If you get confused by the markings on your ruler, put strips of masking tape on the lines you are using. You can change them when you cut on new lines.

Fussy cutting. If you are using feature fabric you may wish to 'fussy cut'. Place a square ruler on the fabric and move around until you feel you have a good 'picture' underneath.

Check that you have the sides of the square on the fabric grain-lines, i.e. parallel or at right angles to the selvedge. Cut out the square. Move to a different part of the fabric and repeat. You will find that the fabric is full of square holes.

Patchwork blocks

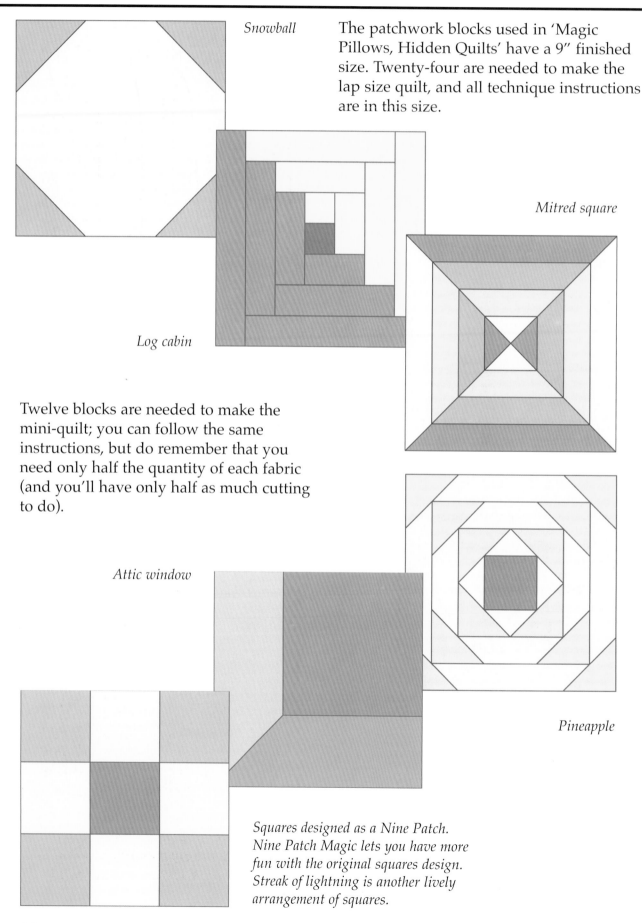

Snowball

The patchwork blocks used in 'Magic Pillows, Hidden Quilts' have a 9" finished size. Twenty-four are needed to make the lap size quilt, and all technique instructions are in this size.

Mitred square

Log cabin

Twelve blocks are needed to make the mini-quilt; you can follow the same instructions, but do remember that you need only half the quantity of each fabric (and you'll have only half as much cutting to do).

Attic window

Pineapple

Squares designed as a Nine Patch. Nine Patch Magic lets you have more fun with the original squares design. Streak of lightning is another lively arrangement of squares.

Each patchwork block is sewn using fast machine techniques, sewing twenty-four multiples of one block to make a lap size quilt. However...

...here you can see that alternating two different blocks throughout the quilt gives you even more interesting patchwork patterns.

Snowball

Simply a square which has its corners replaced with a different fabric. The centre space is great for showing off large fabric prints, or some lovely quilting.

Fabric needed for lap quilt

Snowball centre: 1¾ yards

Snowball corners: 1 yard

Cutting instructions

Four small corner squares are needed for each large square.

Large squares: cut six 9½" width strips of fabric and cut into twenty-four squares. If you are using a large print you may wish to fussy cut (see Hints and tips, p. 14)

Corners: cut nine 3½" width strips of fabric, and cut into ninety-six squares.

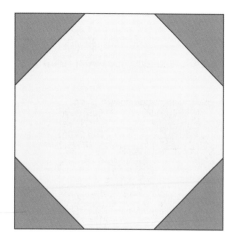

1 On the wrong side of each small square, draw a diagonal line.

2 Right sides together, place a corner square in each corner of a large square, matching raw edges.

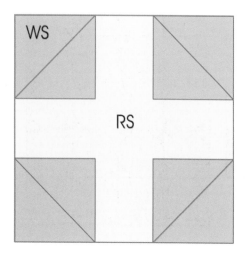

3 Stitch on the diagonal marked line on each corner square. There is no need to break the threads between each corner. Press to bed the stitches.

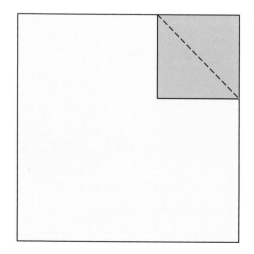

4 At each corner, cut away excess fabric to leave a ¼" seam outside the stitching line.

5 Press corner triangles away from the centre square. Check the block measurement is 9½".

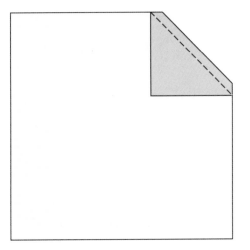

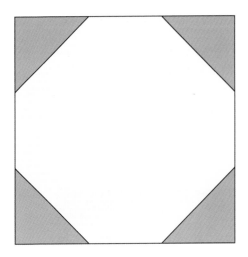

QH Tip

Don't like to waste the cut-off triangles? Sew a second line of stitching ½" outside the marked line on each corner. Cut between the stitched lines. You will now have a half square triangle as a bonus from each corner.

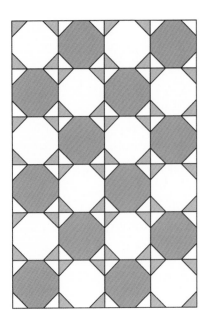

Snowball combines well with other blocks, but even when it's on its own you can ring the changes. Try adding corner triangles to a ready-pieced four-patch; and how would it look if you pieced the triangles before sewing them to the main piece?

Log cabin

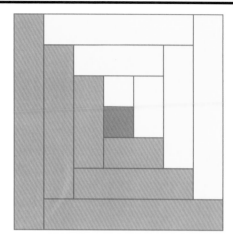

This is one of my favourite patchwork designs, because it is so versatile. Each log cabin is constructed from the centre outwards. Fabric strips are sewn around the centre square. Light fabrics are sewn on one half and dark fabrics on the other, separating the log cabin square into two triangles. This method is fast, as all the twenty-four log cabin squares for your quilt top are worked at the same time.

Fabric needed for lap quilt

Centre: ⅛ yard. Including border of same fabric: 1 yard

Light (L) logs: 1½ yards **or** each light log a different fabric

L1: ⅛ yard **L2:** ¼ yard **L3:** ⅜ yard **L4:** ⅜ yard **L5:** ½ yard **L6:** ½ yard

Dark (D) logs: 1¼ yards **or** each dark log a different fabric

D1: ¼ yard **D2:** ⅜ yard **D3:** ⅜ yard **D4:** ½ yard **D5:** ½ yard **D6:** ⅝ yard

Cutting instructions

Centre square: cut two 2″ wide strips

Logs: cut 1¾″ wide strips

1 Take centre fabric strip and first light log strip, stitch together with a scant ¼″ seam.

2 Gently press away from centre strip. Cut into 2″ pieces at right angles to seam.

3 Take second light log fabric and place right side up under machine presser foot. Insert the needle exactly ¼″ away from fabric edge. Lift presser foot, leaving the needle in the fabric. Position a centre section right side down on the light fabric, matching raw edges.

4 Lower the presser foot and stitch into place with a scant ¼″ seam. Finish sewing with your needle in the fabric just past the patchwork.

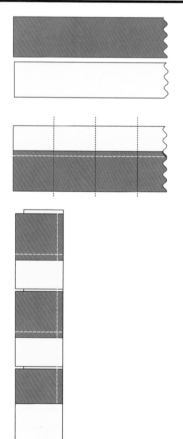

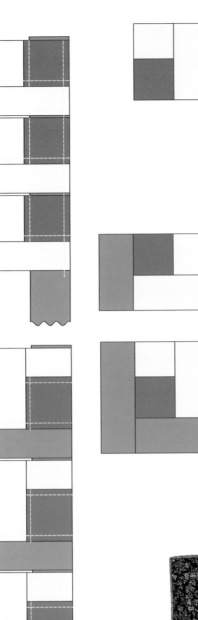

5 Lift the presser foot and position the next centre section. Sew into position and repeat until all the twenty four centres have been sewn onto the second light fabric.

6 Cut apart at right angles to seam line, alongside raw edges. Press seams away from the centre. Check measurement is 2¾".

7 Place the first dark log strip right side up under the presser foot, as you did in step 3. Sew all the patchwork to the dark fabric. Cut apart and again press away from the centre.

8 Add the second dark log (measurement 4") then the third light log.

9 Continue adding light and dark logs until the square is 9½". Note the position of each fabric as it is sewn to the centre.

10 Now comes the fun part: arranging the twenty four log cabin blocks into a design!

Pam Bailey's Log Cabin *shows just how effective this block can be.*

A little inspiration

You've seen the diagrams, but how can you really use the blocks in this book? The next three pages show you just how much can be done with a single block...

Attic Windows provide the perfect frame for Felicity Parsons' Cool Cats *(top left and right), while Pat Boyes'* Log Cabin *(below) offers a different take on this popular block.*

Pineapple Frenzy *(left) by Maggie Baker shows pineapple blocks arranged in the traditional barn-raising design used in log cabin quilts.*

Snowballs *by Kathleen Brennan; the snowball colours were chosen from the border print, which then helps to link all the colours together.*

In Streak of Lightning *by Anne Steinburg colours flow diagonally across the quilt, with the border fabric once again picking up all the colours.*

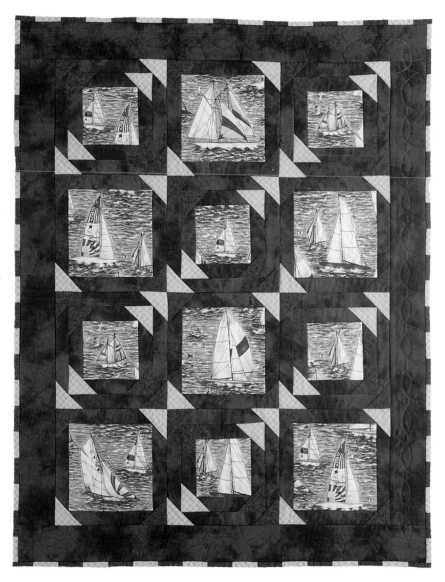

Ships Ahoy *by Karin Hellaby uses fussy cut fabric to make it look like an album quilt, and the easy pineapple technique described on p.26.*

Mitred square

The mitred square gives the optical illusion of depth, if you place the fabric in order of light value from light to dark. It is an intriguing block that simply starts life as strips of fabric.

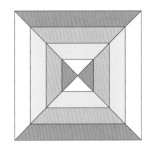

Fabric needed for lap quilt

¾ yard of each of four contrasting fabrics

Cutting instructions

Cut fourteen 1⅝" strips (full width) from each fabric. Try layering the four fabrics, ironing them together to help the layers 'stick' and then cutting the strips.

1 Stitch four fabric strips together, one from each fabric, to make a strip set. Remember to reverse the sewing direction after each strip and use a scant ¼" seam. Repeat to make fourteen strip sets.

2 Press the strip sets towards the dark fabric. Press gently from the front using the non-ironing hand to guide the seams from the back. Check width measurement is 5¼".

3 Place two strip sets right sides together on the cutting board, reversing colours and butting seams.

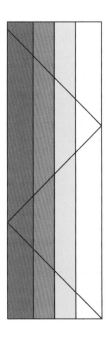

4 Cut into 45-degree triangles. Use a right-angled triangle ruler or the 45-degree angle on a ruler. For the lap quilt you need to cut 48 pairs of triangles. Pin in pairs along one bias edge, checking they are non-identical.

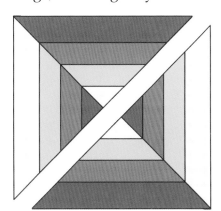

5 Carefully stitch together the pairs of triangles; as you sew along the bias line take care not to stretch the fabric. To prevent distortion, use a walking foot. I like to chain piece one pair after the other.

6 Stitch the pairs into squares, matching seams. Press the diagonal seams open.

7 Arrange the 24 squares into your chosen design.

QH Tip

The 98L Omnigrid triangle is ideal for this: use the line marked 9 on the edge of the strip set.

25

Easy pineapple

I love the look of pineapple patchwork, but I always found it difficult to sew it accurately. When I found this method of stitching triangular corners to log cabin blocks I was thrilled. Not only did I have an easy way of making a 'pineapple' but I also found the log cabin block became more stable when corners were added. The corners are 3D but if you prefer not to have this effect, look at the 'What if?'

Fabric needed for lap quilt

Centre fabric: ⅜ yard

Corners: ¾ yard

Logs: 2½ yards

You may wish to divide the logs into lights and darks arranging them as you would log cabin patchwork.

Cutting instructions

Centres: cut two strips 2¾" wide.

Corners: cut twenty strips 2¾" wide, cut into 288 squares. Fold each square diagonally wrong sides together into a triangle.

Logs: cut 1⅝" wide strips.

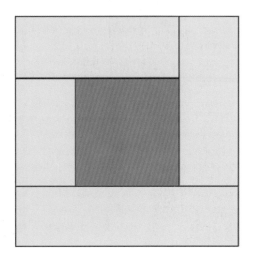

1 Stitch logs around the centre square following instructions for log cabin on p.20 . Make all twenty-four blocks at the same time. First sew the centre strip right sides together to a log strip using a scant ¼". Press towards the log fabric.

Cut twenty-four 2¾" sections. Add logs to all sides of the centre squares. The centre square now has one row of logs stitched to all four sides.

2 Press logs away from the centre. Check measurement of block, which should be 5".

3 Add a corner triangle to each of the four log corners, matching raw edges. To keep the triangles in place while attaching logs, stitch into place ⅛" from the fabric edge, or glue into place using a small amount of Roxanne's Glue Baste-it.

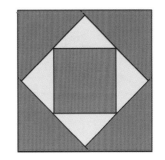

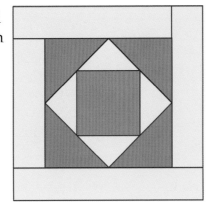

4 Stitch on the next round of logs. Press away from the centre. Check measurement of block, which should be 7¼". Add corners.

5 Proceed until you have completed three rounds of logs. The block should now measure 9½".

6 Arrange the blocks into a design; look at the illustrations for ideas. When sewing the blocks together, press the seams between the blocks open to distribute the extra bulk created by the corners.

What if...

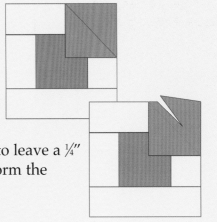

...you don't want 3D corners? Use the corner squares unfolded and proceed as for adding corners in 'snowball' (see p.18). Mark a diagonal line on the wrong side of the squares. Place a square in each corner after a round of logs, right sides together. Stitch on marked line. Trim excess to leave a ¼" seam allowance. Then press the corners out to reform the square.

Picture frame blocks

The centre pineapple can look like a picture frame, and shows off beautiful fabrics to real advantage. Cut 5" squares in a feature fabric. Then add only two rounds of logs and corners to form the 9½" block. Or start with 7¼" squares in a feature fabric and add only one round of logs and corners. The two sizes of 'pictures' can be mixed, as in the *Ships Ahoy* quilt.

To see how this design can look when made up into a quilt, see Ships Ahoy *on p.24.*

The shops are full of beautiful feature fabrics simply crying out for this kind of treatment – but you could also consider other things for your central square. For instance, how about a favourite photo from the family album, scanned into your home computer and printed out on fabric......

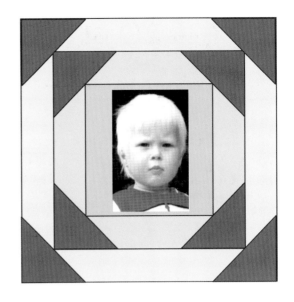

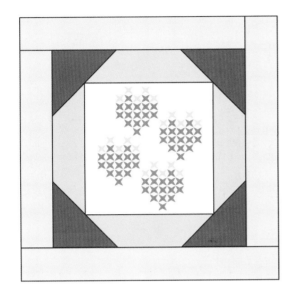

...a favourite piece of embroidery, or cross-stitch – or...

...children's drawings.

And don't forget that other blocks – particularly Snowball (see p. 18) and Attic Window (next page) – are also very suitable as picture frames.

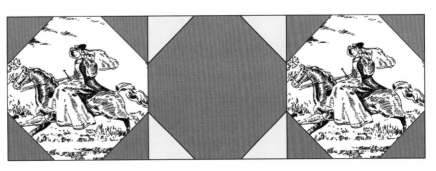

29

Attic Window

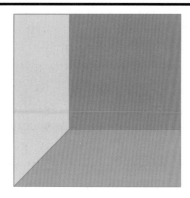

The Attic Window design gives you 'room for a view'. The twenty-four squares are ideal for showing off a special printed fabric, or for placing fabric photographs, kids' drawings and larger motifs. You may need to 'fussy cut' the fabric (see p.15) to get that special view.

Fabric needed for lap quilt

Light: 1 yard

Medium: 1 yard

Dark: 1 yard

Cutting instructions

Light: cut six 3½"-wide strips, cut into twenty-four 10" lengths.

Medium: cut six 3½"-wide strips, cut into twenty-four 10" lengths.

Dark: twenty-four 6½" squares.

1 Place the square right side up. Insert a pin at the bottom left-hand corner ¼" from the two sides. Mark a dot on the wrong side of the fabric where the pin comes through.

2 Stitch a light fabric strip, right sides together, to the correct side of the square. Line up the strip with the top corner and sew to the bottom corner, stopping one stitch short of the ¼" mark. Reverse stitch three or four stitches. You will have at least 4" excess fabric; do not cut off! Press away from the square.

3 Repeat, using a dark strip on the bottom side of the square. Always start sewing from the corner away from the mitre.

4 Press strips away from the square.

QH Tip

You can avoid the marking step if you have a ¼" sewing machine foot that has markings ¼" in front and behind the needle placement.

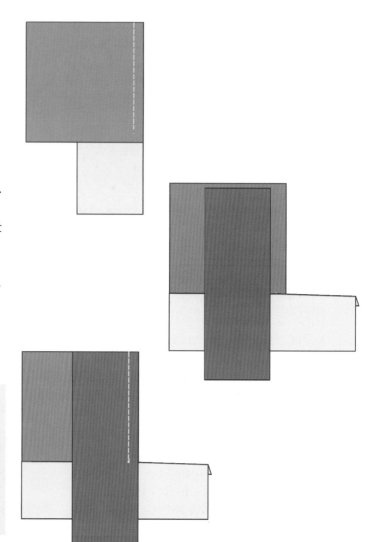

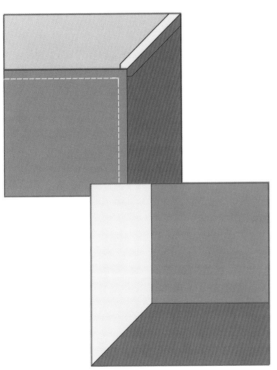

5 The next step is best done on the ironing board. Place the square right side up with the border strips at the top and right side. Left-handers may wish to mirror image this. At the corner, fold the excess side strip under to lie in line with the top strip, forming the mitre. Check the mitre with the 45-degree line on a ruler. Place the pre-heated iron carefully on the 'mitre' and hold for five seconds (the time it takes to slowly say 'got you'). This pressed mark will be your sewing line. Insert a pin near the mitre.

5 Carefully turn the patchwork to the wrong side and move the pin to the reverse side without disturbing the mitre. Add more pins to hold the mitre in place. Stitch on the pressed line, starting at the outside corner and stitching to within one stitch of the inside corner. Reverse stitch to anchor the threads.

6 Check the seam from the right side. It should be flat, with a mitred corner. Trim the seam to ¼". Press the seam open. Check square measurement is 9½"; trim if necessary.

7 When you have sewn all twenty-four attic windows, sew them together following the general instructions.

QH Tips

To help you sew the strips on the correct sides of the square, place them right side up alongside and in line with each other. Then carefully flip the square over onto the strip, and pin.

If you don't like reverse stitching, stop with the needle in the fabric, turn the fabric round to face the stitches you have just sewn, and forward stitch over them.

What if...

...you want sashing between your Attic Window squares? Cut 1" x 9½" strips and sew to the left side of each of eighteen attic windows. Stitch into rows with a sashing-free attic window on the left side of each row. Sew rows together, adding 1" between the rows. I also like to use the same sashing round the whole quilt before adding a narrower border. The finished size should still be about 44" x 63".

Nine patch

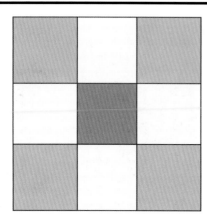

The traditional way of making this block was to cut nine squares and stitch them together. A faster method when making multiple blocks for a quilt is to cut strips, sew them together, cut again and sew them together into nine-patch blocks.

Fabric needed for lap quilt

Light: 1 yard

Medium: 1 yard

Dark: ¼ yard

Cutting instructions

For a 9″ finished block:

Light fabric: cut eight 3½″ strips

Medium fabric: cut eight 3½″ strips

Dark fabric: cut two 3½″ strips

1 Stitch the strips into two different strip sets; make four pairs of strips altogether.

2 Press seams in each strip towards the dark fabric(s).

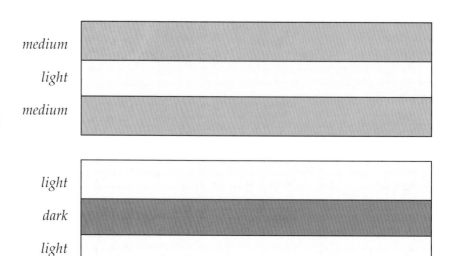

medium
light
medium

light
dark
light

3 Cut 3½″ sections from each strip set, at right angles to the seam.

4 Stitch the pieces together. Press seams to one side.

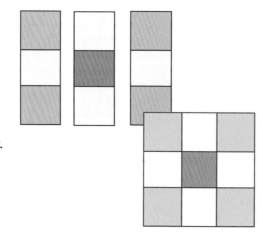

A few examples...

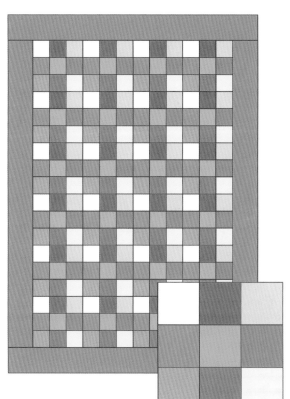

What if...

...you changed the position of the light, medium and dark strips in the strip set?

...you used nine different fabrics?

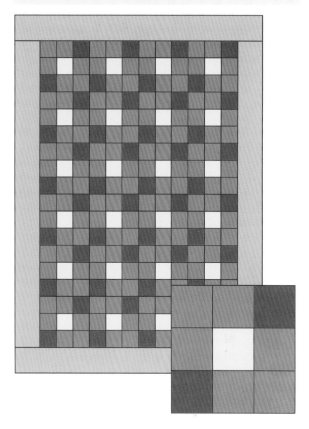

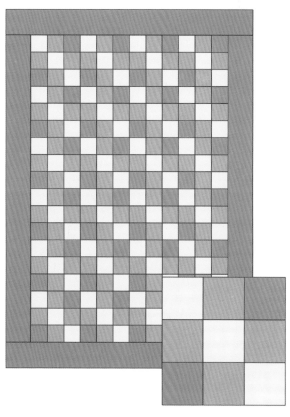

Nine patch magic

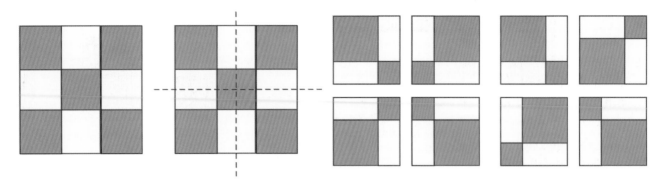

Show people one of these nine patch magic designs and ask them how it started off. No one will guess it was a simple nine-patch block!

Fabric needed for lap quilt

You will need approximately 3 yards of fabric. For the simplest arrangement (as above) choose two contrasting fabrics. Fabricoholics may wish to choose up to nine (see below).

Cutting instructions

Cut 3¾" wide strips of fabric in darks and lights.

1 Sew strips together into different strip sets. Each set will have three strips.

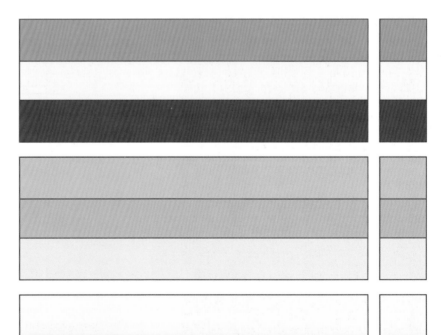

2 Press each strip set towards the dark fabrics. At right angles to strip set seams, straighten one side and cut 3¾" sections (i.e. a three-square strip).

3 Sew three sections together to form a nine patch. Press. You should have a square slightly larger than 10".

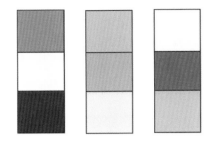

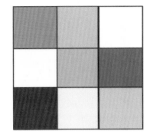

4 Placing the 5" ruler line on the edges of the square, cut through the centre of the nine-patch square in both directions, there may be a small strip of waste fabric to discard, to make four smaller squares (5"). Four sewn together make a 9½" block.

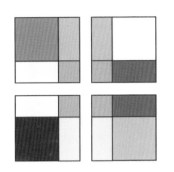

5 Arrange the squares (8 x 24) until you have a pleasing design. Stitch into quilt top.

Two examples (below and right) of nine-patch magic in action.

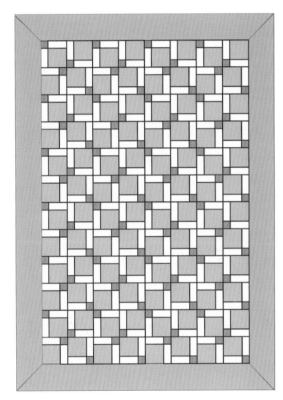

What if...

...the centre square was a medium, or one colour?

...several darks and several lights were used?

...you combined 'light' and 'dark' nine patches?

Streak of lightning

At first sight this simple but effective design looks as if it is made from many squares sewn together. With this quick method, strips of fabric are sewn together and then cut at right angles to give you strips of squares. The streaks of diagonal colour across the quilt give the impression of lightning.

Cutting instructions for lap quilt

Choose eight fabrics.

Cut two 5" wide strips approx. 42" long from each fabric.

1 Make two strip sets, each containing a strip from each of the eight fabrics. Each set must have the fabrics sewn in the same order. To make a strip set, sew the strips together along their length using a scant ¼" seam. Reverse the sewing direction after each strip to prevent a curve forming in the set.

2 Press all the seams in one direction. I prefer to do this from the front of the patchwork. I sweep the side of the iron across the seams, using my non-ironing hand to direct the seams. Check that the seams are stretched out, with no hidden creases.

3 Fold a strip set in half along a seam. I like to work with the wrong sides out.

4 Straighten one side at right angles to the seams.

5 Cut 5" wide strips. Each strip will have eight different fabric squares within its length. You will need 12 strips for a lap size quilt.

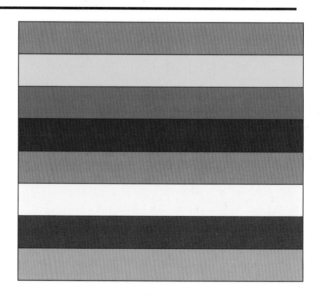

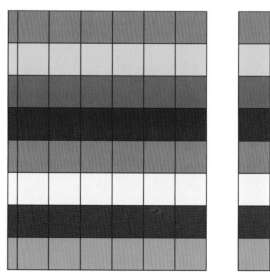

6 Leave two strips open. Sew the remaining ten strips into separate tubes, by stitching the short ends together. This is quicker if you chain stitch, one seam after the other.

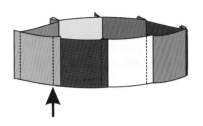

7 Lay the first strip out. Take one of the tubes and open out the seam between fabrics 1 and 2, lay alongside the first strip. Take a second tube and open out the seam between fabrics 2 and 3, lay alongside the second strip. Continue until you have laid out the strips to form the pattern on the left.

8 Stitch the strips together, Use the 'nestle and wrestle' technique (see p.14) for matching the intersecting seams. Remember to reverse sewing direction after each seam.

9 Press the quilt top. You may prefer to press horizontal seams open to distribute bulk.

QH Tip

To prevent the strips from becoming distorted, straighten the strip set after every fourth cut. Do this by checking that your straight edge is at right angles to the seams.

A quillow cushion cover design using the Streak of Lightning block.

What if...

...you want a brick effect? Instead of unpicking the seam separating fabric squares you can cut the square in half on alternate strips. The seams are staggered, and no perfect seam matching is required.

37

Nine-patch variations

So far all the 9″ blocks have been of one technique only.

The 9″ blocks can be subdivided to give more versatility – three squares across and three squares down, forming nine separate units. Each unit is a 3″ square. I have used some simple patchwork in each of the nine units, and some quick sewing techniques are explained in the following pages. The basic units are:

 Plain square

A square divided into two rectangles

 Four patch square

Pinwheels

 Half square triangle

Quarter square triangle

These 3″ units can be used individually or in combinations to make nine patch blocks, as you can see in the examples shown here. There are many more that you can design for yourself.

38

Rectangles & Four-patch

A two-colour strip set is used to make both rectangles and four-patch units.

Making the strip set

1 Cut two 2" strips in two contrasting fabrics.

2 Stitch along the length using a ¼" seam.

3 Press along the seam to bed the stitches.

4 From the front, sweep the side of the iron from light to dark fabric, making sure that no folds occur at the seam when pressing.

Rectangles

Cut 3½" squares from the two-coloured strip.

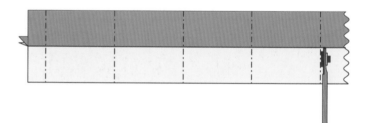

Four patch

1 Fold the strip in half, crease, and cut on the crease line. Fit right sides together, reversing the light and dark fabrics so that the seams nestle against one another.

2 Rotary cut to straighten one end at right angles to the seam. Cut 2" pieces.

3 Stitch together, opposing the seam and making the pairs 'nestle and wrestle' for a perfect match (see p.14). Use a flower pin to guide the fabric towards the needle, and chain stitch each pair, one after the other.

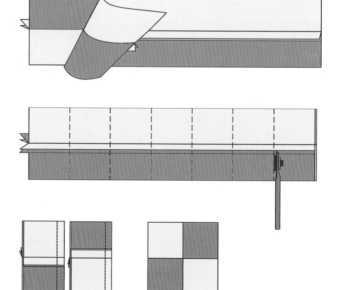

40

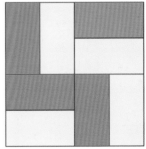

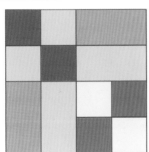

Formulae

Two rectangles in a square

For the cut strip, take finished measurement of square, divide by 2, and add ½″, e.g.:

3″ square: $3 \div 2 = 1\frac{1}{2} + \frac{1}{2} = 2″$ cut strips in two colours

9″ square: $9 \div 2 = 4\frac{1}{2} + \frac{1}{2} = 5″$ cut strips in two colours

Four patch in a square

As above. When cutting the strip set into sections, use the measurement of one of the original cut strips.

Half-square triangles & Pinwheels

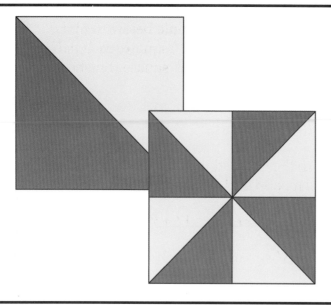

Cutting instructions

For 3″ half-square triangles, use two contrasting fabrics, iron right sides together, and spray starch (if necessary) to help them adhere.

Cut strips 3⅞″ wide, and cut into squares.

You should now have two matching, contrasting squares. Keep them exactly together, as they have been cut. Each pair of squares will give you two 3″ finished half square triangle units.

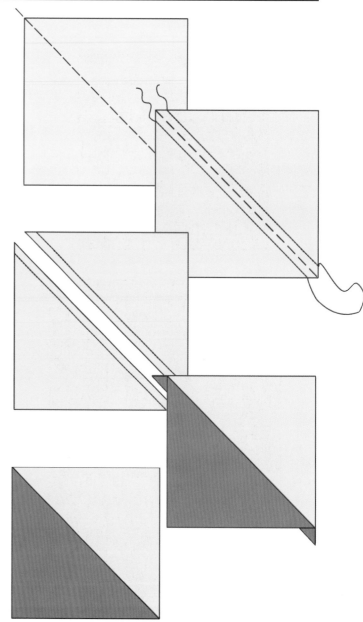

1 Proceed with the squares kept together in their contrasting pairs. Mark a diagonal line on the wrong side of the lightest square.

2 Stitch ¼″ away from the marked line. Sew one side of the line, pull the unit away from the presser foot without breaking the thread, and then sew down the other side again ¼″ away from the line.

3 Press to bed the stitches.

4 Cut on the marked line to divide the square into two equal triangles.

5 Open each triangle to magically reveal squares with two contrasting triangles.

6 Gently press the centre seam towards the dark fabric. Take care not to stretch the seam while you are pressing. Cut off the 'ears' (the excess fabric sticking out from the edges of the square).

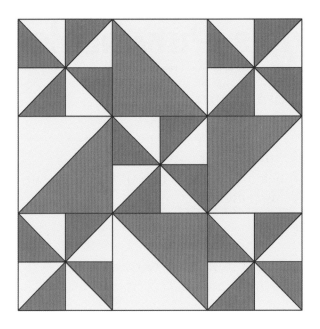

Pinwheels

...are four half-square triangles stitched together. Use the formula below to make the pinwheels. For a 3" square, each half square triangle is a 1½" square (finished sizes).

Cutting formula

Take the finished measurement of the square and add ⁷⁄₈", e.g.:

For a 1½" square   1½ + ⅞ =   2⅜"

For a 3" square   3 + ⅞ =   3⅞"

For a 4½" square   4½ + ⅞ =   5⅜"

For a 9" square   9 + ⅞ =   9⅞"

Pinwheels in various sizes

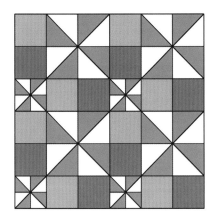

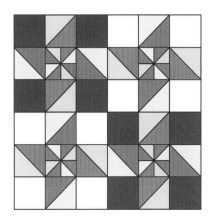

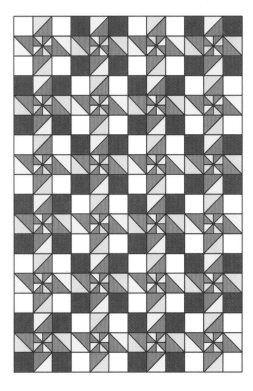

Quarter-square triangles

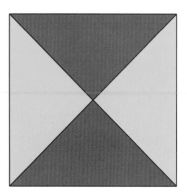

Cutting instructions

For 3" quarter-square triangles

Take two contrasting fabrics, iron right sides together, spray starch if necessary to help them adhere to one another.

Cut a fabric strip 4¼" wide, then cut into squares.

You now have two matching contrasting squares. Keep them together exactly as they have been cut. Each pair of squares will give you two 3" finished quarter-square triangle blocks.

1 Follow steps 1-6 as in Half-square triangles (see p.42).

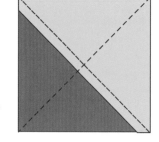

2 On the wrong side of one half square triangle mark a diagonal line which crosses over the seam line from corner to corner.

3 Place this square right sides together with an unmarked half square triangle, reversing the colours against one another. Nestle the centre seams and pin diagonally where they fit.

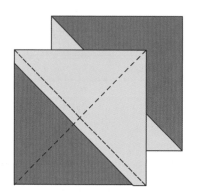
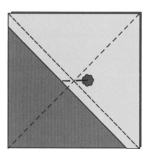

4 Starting from the direction where you will oppose the top centre seam (this will push it into the seam below for a perfect matching centre) sew either side of the marked line.

5 Press to bed the stitches.

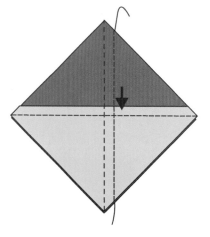

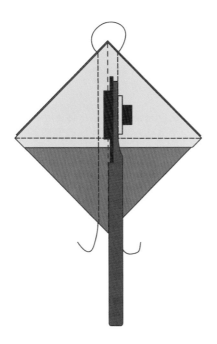

6 Cut on the diagonal line. Open up two squares.

7 Gently press the seam in one direction, admiring your perfectly matched centre points.

Cutting formula

Take the finished measurement of the square and add 1¼″, e.g.:

For a 3″ square   3 + 1¼ =   4¼″

For a 9″ square   9 + 1¼ =   10¼″

A quilt design featuring quarter-square triangles mixed with plain squares.

Perfect pairings

Many of the quillows and quilts in this book use two or more different blocks to create a particular effect. If you're looking for inspiration, one of these suggested designs may help – or you could study some of the photographs on other pages!

The examples on this page all use nine-patch; but notice how combining it with Attic Window (left) gives an extra sense of depth and perspective to the design.

*Nine-patch combined with
Snowball (left and below)*

*A more complex nine-patch
design (above), and a
combination of a simple nine-
patch with Half-square Triangles
(right).*

Quillow projects

All the quilts in this book are fast and fun! They allow you to be creative in a short time as they are rotary cut and machine pieced.

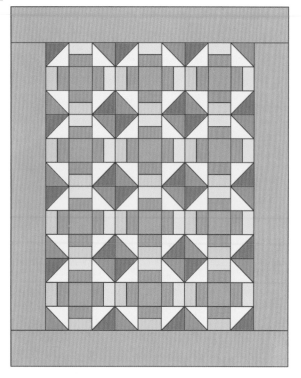

Like the suggested designs on these pages, the projects that follow on pp. 50–71 are to help you get started, and they are arranged in order of difficulty.

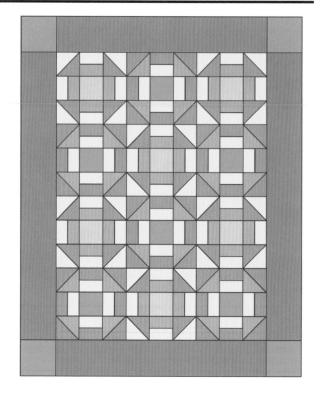

The quilters who made the projects chose one of my many patterns, and then chose the fabric they wanted to use and the quilt size they wished to make.

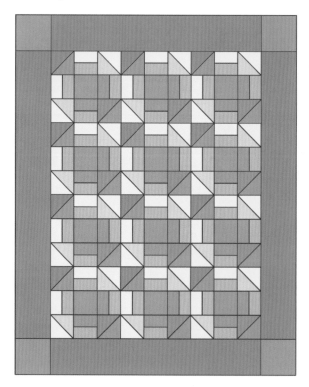

I hope you enjoy working with the projects as much as the original makers.

On page 96 you will find the company names and addresses of the fabric contributors, so that you can contact them if you see a fabric that inspires you!

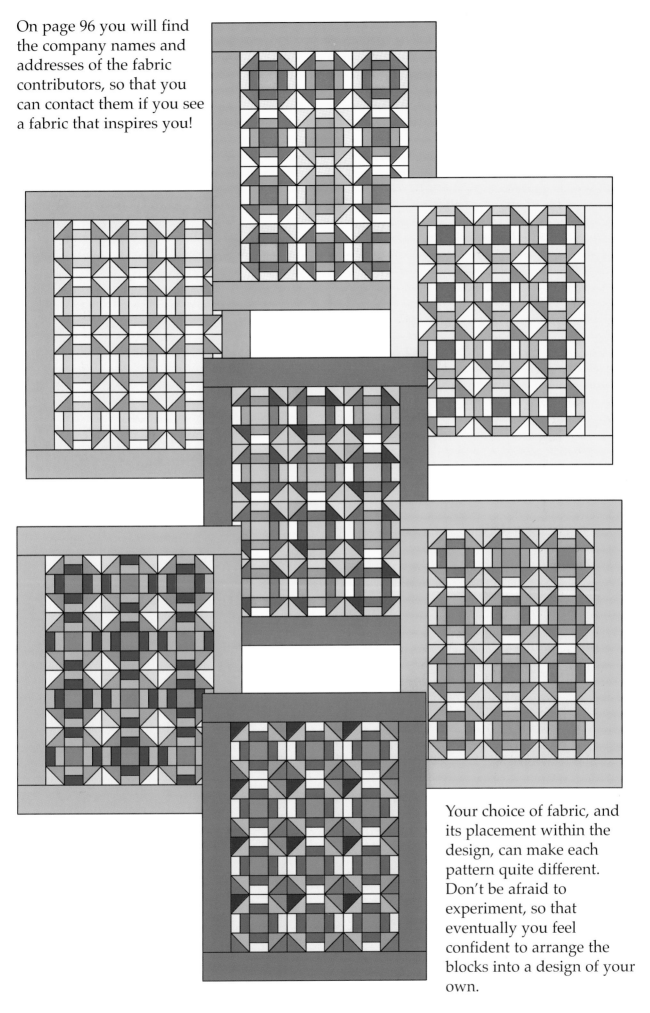

Your choice of fabric, and its placement within the design, can make each pattern quite different. Don't be afraid to experiment, so that eventually you feel confident to arrange the blocks into a design of your own.

Bright and Breezy, really easy

Bright and Breezy *by Teresa Wardlaw*

Fabric needed for mini quilt

7 fabrics: ¼ yard each

Green: ¾ yard, which includes binding

Blue: 1¼ yards, which includes border

Cutting instructions

12 Nine patch blocks (see p. 32)

Using all nine fabrics, cut one 3½" strip from each.

Border

Blue: cut 4 x 3½" strips

6 Nine patch blocks

1 Make 3 strip sets, each using the 3½" strips from 9 different fabrics.

2 From each strip set cut 12 x 3½" pieces at right angles to seams.

3 Stitch one piece from each colour set into a nine patch block.

4 Stitch 12 nine patch blocks into quilt top.

5 Add a 3½" border.

Teresa made a reversible wrap around pillow for her Bright and Breezy *flannel quilt. The quilt is layered with a cotton wadding and machine quilted. It makes an ideal present for a baby; you could even use the cushion cover as a changing mat!*

50

Fabric needed for mini quilt

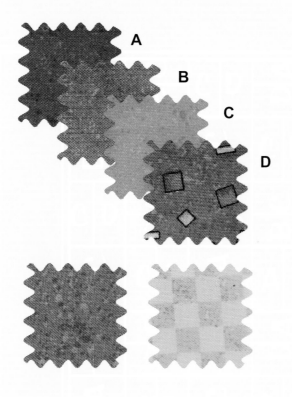

Steps *by Anne Smith*

Blue (A), Lavender (B), Pink (C) and Patterned turquoise (D): ½ yard each.

Yellow: ¼ yard

Mottled turquoise: 1½ yards, includes enough for binding

Cutting instructions

Cut 6 x 2¾" strips in each of blue, lavender, pink and patterned turquoise.

Border

Yellow: cut 4 x ¾" strips

Turquoise: cut 4 x 4½" strips

Anne made a wrap-around pillow. The quilt and pillow were hand quilted.

1 For Rectangles see p.40. Stitch together pairs of strips, right sides together, along their length:

3 pairs blue(A) / lavender (B)

3 pairs lavender (B) / pink (C)

3 pairs pink (C) / patterned turquoise (D)

3 pairs patterned turquoise (D) / blue (A)

2 Press towards darker fabric.

3 Cut each double strip into 30 x 5" squares. Then stitch the squares together into horizontal rows. Alternate the seams horizontally and vertically, placing colours as shown. Stitch rows into quilt top. Press.

4 Add ¾" yellow strips folded double as a flat piping strip, then sew on the mottled turquoise 4½" strips as the outer border.

Desert Jewels

Desert Jewels *by Pippa Moss. Pippa made her quilt into a quillow using the traditional method. The pillow has a pineapple design, and both quilt and pillow were machine quilted.*

Fabric needed for lap quilt

Light: 2 yards, includes border

Brown: ¾ yard

Pink: ¾ yard

Border stripe: 1¾ yards, includes binding

6 Jewel fabrics: ⅛ yard of each

Cutting instructions

Light: cut 11 x 3¾" strips

Brown: cut 5 x 3¾" strips

Pink: cut 5 x 3¾" strips

Jewels: cut one 3¾" strip in each fabric

Border

Light: cut 5 x 1½" strips

Stripe: cut 6 x 3½" strips

Nine Patch Magic squares (see p. 34)

1 Sew strip sets (brown/light/pink – 5 sets).

2 Cut jewel strips in half and make 6 half strip sets (approx. 20" long) light/ jewel/light (6 half sets).

3 Cut 3¾" sections from each strip set. Stitch into 24 nine patches. Press.

4 Cut each nine patch into 4 x 5" blocks (96). Arrange as shown in quilt above.

5 Add a 1½" light border.

6 Add a 3½" striped border.

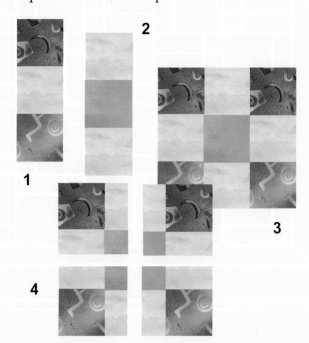

Fabric needed for lap quilt

Yellow: ¾ yard

Yellow print: ¾ yard

Blue: ¾ yard

Blue/Yellow print: ¾ yard

Dark (includes borders): 1¼ yards

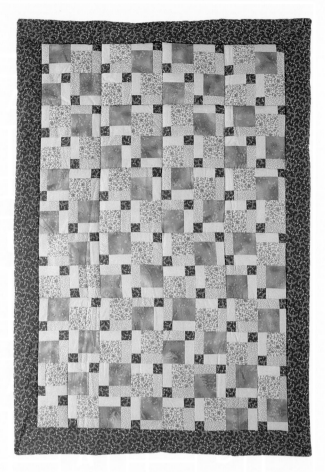

Summer Skies *by John Hazon*

Cutting instructions

Yellow: cut 6 x 3¾" strips

Yellow print: cut 6 x 3¾" strips

Blue: cut 6 x 3¾" strips

Blue/Yellow print: cut 6 x 3¾" strips

Dark: cut 3 x 3¾" strips

Borders

Dark: cut 6 x 4½" strips

1 Using Nine Patch Magic squares (see p. 34), sew strip sets (three sets in each colourway). Press.

2 Cut 24 x 3¾" sections from each colourway.

3 Stitch into nine patch. Press.

4 Cut each nine patch into 4 x 5" blocks.

5 Arrange blocks as shown.

6 Add a 4½" striped border.

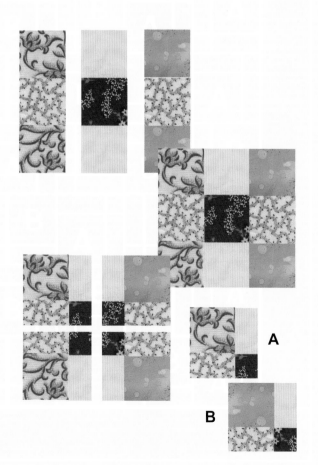

A

B

John made a quillow using no-binding method.
He used a high loft polyester wadding and machine quilting.

Love Story

Fabric needed for wall hanging

Picture print: 1 yard

Light blue: ¼ yard

Blue: ¼ yard

Pink: ¼ yard

Red: ¼ yard

2 Clarets: ¼ yard of each

Print: 1¾ yards for border and binding

Cutting instructions

6 Snowball blocks (see p. 18)

Picture print: fussy cut 6 x 9½" squares

Claret A: cut one 3½" strip, cut into 12 squares

Claret B: cut one 3½" strip, cut into 12 squares

6 Four patch blocks (see p. 40)

Cut a 5" strip from each of the four fabrics

Border

Print: cut 4 x 3½" strips

Love Story, made by Pat Matthes. The picture fabric in the snowball centres depicts 19th-century lovers, and the blocks were arranged in the love story sequence.

Four patch blocks

1 Stitch together pairs of 5" strips along their length, right sides together:

1 pair light blue/blue

1 pair pink/red

2 Press towards the darker fabric. Cut 5" sections.

3 Stitch into 6 squares, stitching alternating blocks together as shown above.

4 Add a 3½" border.

Fabric needed for mini-quilt size

Lights (5): 1¼ yards in all, includes border

Print: 1 yard, includes border

Blue: ¼ yard

Dark blue: ¼ yard

Pink: ¼ yard

Dark pink: 1 yard, includes binding

Cutting instructions

12 blocks

Light: cut 4 x 2" strips and 4 x 3⅞" strips

Print: cut one 3½" strip, cut into 12 squares

Blue: cut 2 x 3⅞" strips

Dark blue: cut 2 x 3⅞" strips

Pink: cut 2 x 2" strips

Dark pink: cut 2 x 2" strips

Borders

Light: cut 5 x 1½" strips

Print: cut 6 x 3½" strips

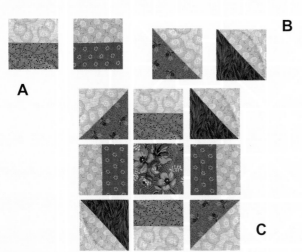

Pam made a wrap-around pillow. Both quilt and pillow are hand quilted.

Memory Rose *by Pam Bailey*

A Rectangles (see p. 40)

1 Stitch together pairs of 2" strips along their length, right sides together

   2 pairs light / pink

   2 pairs light / dark pink

   Press towards the darker fabric.

2 Cut each colourway into 24 x 3½" rectangles to make 48 rectangle units, 4 for each 9" block.

B Half square triangles (see p. 42)

3 Layer 2 light with 2 x pale blue 3⅞" strips right sides together. Layer 2 light with 2 x dark blue 3⅞" strips right sides together.

4 Cut each colourway into 12 x 3⅞" squares.

5 Stitch into 48 half-square triangles, check each measures 3½".

C Block construction

6 Stitch units into rows, and rows into block. Make 12 blocks. Stitch into quilt top.

7 Add a 1½" light border.

8 Add a 3½" print border.

Market Crossing

Market Crossing *by Charmaine Sampson.*
Charmaine backed her quilt with a red polyester
fleece and quilted hearts into the red squares using
big stitch.

Fabric needed for lap quilt

Light: 1 yard

Red: ¾ yard

Mid blue: 1
yard, includes
binding

Dark blue: 2½
yards

Cutting instructions

24 blocks

Light: cut 2 x 3½" strips, cut into 24 squares,
and 5 x 3⅞" strips

Red: cut 4 x 3½" strip, cut into 48 squares

Mid blue: cut 2 x 3½" strips, cut into 24
squares

Dark blue: cut 2 x 3½" strip, cut into 24
squares, and 5 x 3⅞" strips

Border

Red: cut 4 x 4½" squares

Dark blue: cut 6 x 4½" strips

Market Crossing is made from two
alternating blocks. Each block is made up
of squares and half square triangle units
which form a nine patch.

Half square triangles (see p.42)

(see p.42)

1 Layer 5 light and 5 dark blue 3⅞" strips
  in pairs, right sides together.

2 Cut into 48 x 3⅞" squares. Stitch into 96
  half square triangles, check each
  measures 3½".

3 Stitch into rows, alternating 3½" squares
  with half-square triangles.

4 Stitch rows into 12 A blocks and 12 B
  blocks.

Border

5 Add side strips.

6 Add red squares to either end of top and
  bottom border strips. Add to quilt.

Fabric needed for lap quilt

Print: 1¼ yards, includes border

Black: 2 yards, includes border

Purple: ½ yard

Pink: ¼ yard

Cutting instructions

Four patch (see p. 40)

Print: cut 2 x 5"strips

Black: cut 2 x 5" strips

Chain block (see p. 39)

Black: cut 4 x 3½" strips, cut into 48 squares, plus 7 x 2" strips

Purple: cut 5 x 2" strips

Pink: cut 2 x 2" strips

Border

Black: cut 5 x 2" strips

Print: cut 6 x 3½" strips

Midnight Garden: *by Heather Langdon. Heather made a quillow using the 'no binding' method; she used a needled polyester wadding and machine quilting. The quillow cover (left) uses only the Irish chain blocks.*

12 Four patch blocks

1 Layer together 2 pairs of 5" strips, right sides together.

2 Stitch along their length. Press towards black. Cut 5" sections.

3 Stitch into 12 blocks.

12 Chain blocks

4 Layer 2 pink and 2 black 2" strips in pairs, right sides together.

5 Stitch into 12 x 3½" four patch units.

6 Layer 5 purple and 5 black 2" strips in pairs, right sides together.

7 Stitch into 48 x 3½" four patch units.

8 Stitch units into rows alternating four patch with a black 3½" square. Stitch 3 rows into a block. Make 12 blocks.

9 Stitch alternating four patch and chain blocks together into quilt top. Add black and then print borders.

Through the Portholes *by Karin Hellaby*

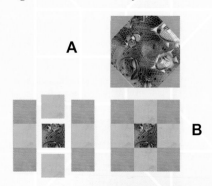

A

B

C

Karin made a wrap-around pillow for her lap quilt. Wool wadding was used; both quilt and pillow were machine quilted on a long-arm machine by Jan Chandler.

Fabric needed for lap quilt

Fish: 2 yards, includes binding

Yellow: ½ yard

Orange: 1 yard

Border: 1 yard

Cutting instructions

12 Snowballs (see p. 18)

Fish: cut 3 x 9½" strips, cut into 12 squares

Orange: cut 4 x 3½" strips, cut into 48 squares

12 Nine patch (see p. 32)

Yellow: cut 4 x 3½" strips, cut 24 squares

Orange: cut 4 x 3½" strips

Fish: fussy cut 12 x 3½" squares (C)

Border

Orange check: cut 6 x 4½" strips

Fish corners: cut 4 x 4½" squares

12 Snowball blocks (A)

12 Nine patch blocks (B)

1 Use 3½" strips to make two strip sets in orange/ yellow/orange. Cut 24 x 3½" sections which are used as outer strips of nine patch. Stitch yellow and fish 3½" squares into middle strip of nine patch. Stitch strips together to make nine patch blocks. Make 12 blocks.

2 Stitch alternating snowball and nine patch blocks into quilt top.

Border (C)

3 Stitch side strips to quilt top. Add fussy cut fish squares to either end of top and bottom border strips. Stitch to quilt.

Fabric needed for lap quilt

Gecko: 1 yard, add extra if fussy cutting

Orange: ½ yard

Blue: ½ yard

Claret: ½ yard

Print: ½ yard

Border print: 1¾ yards, includes binding

Cutting instructions

12 Snowball blocks (see p.30)

Gecko: cut 3 x 9½" strips, cut into 12 squares

Claret: cut 4 x 3½" strips, cut into 48 squares

12 Chain blocks (see p.39)

Orange: cut 4 x 3½" strips, cut into 48 squares

Blue: cut 5 x 2" strips

Print: cut 5 x 2" strips

Border stripe

cut 6 x 4½" strips

12 Snowball Blocks (A)

12 Chain blocks (B)

1 Layer 5 blue and 5 print 2" strips right sides together in pairs.

2 Cut 60 x 3½" four patch units.

3 Sew units into squares

4 Stitch four patch squares to orange squares to create rows.

5 Stitch 3 rows into a block; make 12 blocks

6 Alternating snowball and chain blocks, stitch into quilt top.

Border

7 Add a 4½" border stripe.

Go Go Gecko *by Pat Mathes*

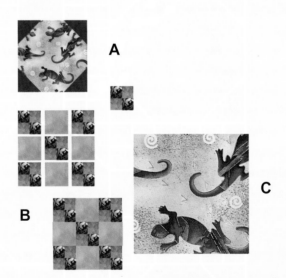

A

B

C

Pat made a slip-in pillow (right). The quilt is backed with a turquoise polyester fleece, and Crow Foot quilting (C) is used to give the effect of animal footprints going across the patchwork.

59

Star Path

Star Path *by Marion Barnes.*

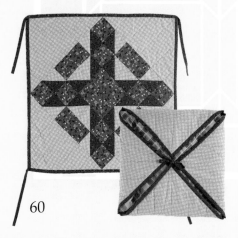

Marion made a wrap-around pillow. The pillow and quilt were hand quilted.

Fabric needed for lap quilt

Light: 1 yard
Red: 1½ yards
Blue print: ¾ yard
Green: ¼ yard
Navy: ¼ yard

Cutting instructions

12 Stars

Light: cut 4 x 3½"strips, cut into 48 squares; cut 5 x 3⅞" strips

Red, navy, green (from each): cut one 3½" strip, cut into 4 squares. Cut one 3⅞" strip.

12 alternating blocks

Light: cut 2 x 3⅞" strips

Blue print: cut 5 x 3½" strips, cut into 60 squares

Red: cut 2 x 3⅞" strips

Border

Red: cut 6 x 4½" strips

12 Star blocks (see p. 38)

1 Layer pairs of 3⅞" strips right sides together using light/red, light/navy, light/green.

2 Cut each colour into 8 x 3⅞"squares. Stitch into 48 x half-square triangles. Sew into blocks with 3½" squares.

3 Make four star blocks in each colour.

12 Alternating blocks (see p. 38)

4 Layer two light with two red 3⅞" strips, in pairs, right sides together. Cut into 24 x 3⅞" squares.

5 Stitch into 48 half-square triangles. Sew into blocks with 3½" blue squares. Make 12 blocks

6 Stitch alternating blocks together into quilt top.

Border

7 Add a 4½" border.

Fabric needed for a lap quilt

Light blue: 1½ yards

Royal blue: ¾ yard

Greens (4): ½ yard of each

Multi: 1¼ yards

Cutting instructions

Light blue: cut 13 x 3⅞" strips

Royal blue: cut 5 x 3⅞" strips

Greens: cut 2 x 3⅞" strips of each

Multi: cut 2 x 3½ strips, cut into 24 squares

Borders

Multi: cut 6 x 4½" strips

Spring into Suffolk is made from 24 identical nine patch squares.

Apart from the centre square every unit in the nine patch is made from half square triangles.

Half square triangles (see p. 42)

(see p. 42)

1 Layer 5 royal blue and 5 light blue 3⅞" strips, right sides together. Cut into 48 x 3⅞" squares. Stitch into 96 half square triangles. Check each half square triangle measures 3½".

2 Layer 8 green and 8 light blue 3⅞" strips, right sides together. From each colour way cut 12 x 3⅞" squares. Stitch into 96 half square triangles, 24 in each colour way. Check each half square triangle measures 3½".

3 Stitch 3 units into a rows, and 3 rows into a block. Make 24 blocks.

4 Stitch 24 blocks together into quilt top.

5 Add a 4½" multi border.

Spring into Suffolk *by Liz Powell.*

Liz made her quilt top into a quillow using the 'no binding' method.

Ships Ahoy!

Ships Ahoy! *by Karin Hellaby*

Fabric needed for wall hanging

Picture fabric: 1 yard

Blue: 1½ yards, includes border

Red: ¾ yard, includes binding

Yellow: ¾ yard, includes binding

Cutting instructions

12 Pineapple blocks (see p.26)

Picture: fussy cut 6 x 5" and 6 x 7¼" squares

Blue: cut 1⅝" strips.

Red: cut 5 x 2¼" strips, cut into 72 squares

Yellow: cut 5 x 2¼" strips, cut into 72 squares

12 Pineapple blocks (see p.26)

1 Use 6 x 7¼" squares. Add a strip frame and corners; the corners are unfolded.

2 Use 6 x 5" squares. Add two strip frames and corners, the corners are unfolded.

3 Stitch alternating blocks together as shown. Add a 4½" blue border.

4 *Ships Ahoy!* was machine quilted with a free motion design in the block centres, in the ditch around each square, and with a border design. A firm needled polyester wadding was used as it is a wall hanging.

Binding

5 Stitch 4 red and yellow 2½" strips into a strip set, alternating colours. Press. Cut 2½" pieces at right angles to seams. Join to make binding strips. Stitch to sides first, then top and bottom.

Fabric needed for lap quilt

Light mauve: 2 yards

Pink: ½ yard

Turquoise: 1½ yards, includes border, binding

Purple: 1 yard

Dragonflies: 1 yard

Cutting Instructions

12 Nine patch blocks (see p. 32)

Light mauve: cut 4 x 3½" strips

Pink: cut 4 x 3½" strips

Dragonflies: cut one 3½" strip

12 Pineapple blocks (see p. 26)

Light mauve: cut 1⅝" strips

Purple: cut 9 x 2¾" strips

Turquoise: cut 4 x 2¾" strips

Borders

Turquoise: cut 6 x 1" strips

Dragonflies: cut 6 x 3½" strips

12 Nine patch blocks (A)

1 Use 3½" strips in three fabrics to make two different strip sets.

   Pink / mauve / pink (2 sets)
   Mauve / dragonfly / mauve (1 set)

2 Cut off 3½" sections and sew into nine patch blocks.

12 Pineapple blocks (B)

All corners have been made with folded squares.

3 Stitch alternating blocks together as shown.

4 Add a 1" folded turquoise border.

5 Add a 3½" dragonfly border.

Dragonfly Flutter *by Dorothy Kennedy*

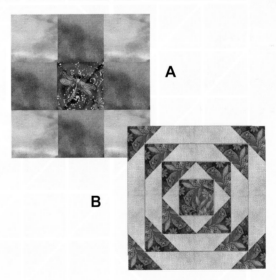

A

B

Dorothy made her quilt top into a quillow, using the traditional method. A low loft polyester wadding was used in the quilt and the pillow so that it could be finely hand quilted before the binding was added.

Rainbow Pinwheels

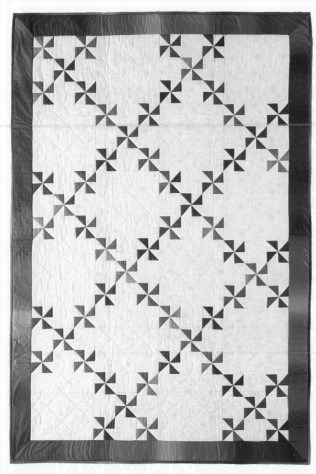

Nine patch pinwheels alternate with plain squares to give a chain effect and space for a lovely quilting pattern. The quilt uses Aurora fabric, one of several that provide a continuous variation of colour across their width.

Rainbow Pinwheels, pieced by Janet Last and quilted by Jan Chandler. Janet made a slip-in pillow (below right).

Fabric needed

Cream: 2 yards

Aurora fabric: 2½ yards, includes border and binding

Cutting instructions

Cream: cut 3 x 9½" strips, cut into 12 squares; cut 4 x 3½" strips, cut into 48 squares; and then cut 8 x 2⅜" strips for pinwheels.

Aurora fabric: cut 8 x 2⅜" strips for pinwheels.

Pinwheels (see p. 43)

Each pinwheel is made from four 1½" half square triangles using the cream and Aurora 2⅜" strips.

1 Cut 120 squares in each fabric.

2 Make 60 pinwheel squares

3 Stitch 5 pinwheel squares with 4 x 3½" cream squares to make a block.

4 Sew three units into three horizontal rows. Press seam to cream square.

5 Sew rows together into a block. Each block should measure 9½".

6 Stitch large cream squares alternating with pinwheel blocks into quilt top.

7 Add a border of Aurora fabric.

Fabric needed for lap quilt

Light: ½ yard

Mottled turquoise: ½ yard

Mottled green: 2 yards, includes borders and binding

Dark: ½ yard

Purple: ½ yard

Pink: ½ yard

The batik fabrics are very variable in colour; much of the interest here comes from the contrast between the lightest and darkest.

Cutting instructions

12 Nine patch blocks (see p. 32)

Pink: cut 4 x 3½" strips

Purple: cut 4 x 3½" strips

Dark: cut one 3½" strip

12 Mitred Square blocks (see p. 25)

Cut 7 x ⅝" strips each in light, mottled turquoise, mottled green and dark

Border

Mottled green: cut 6 x 4½" strips

12 Nine patch blocks

1 Use 3½" strips in three fabrics to make two different strip sets:

Turquoise/pink/turquoise (2 sets)

Pink/dark/pink (1 set)

2 Cut off 3½" sections and sew into nine patch blocks.

12 Mitred Square blocks

3 Make 7 strip sets in four fabrics using 1⅝" strips.

4 Stitch alternating blocks together as shown.

5 Add a 4½" border.

Batik Beauty *by Helen Hazon*

Helen made a slip-in pillow for her quilt. She used cotton wadding in both the quilt and pillow. Machine quilting was done in the ditch so as not to distract from the optical illusion of curves created by the patchwork lines.

Cobwebs in the Windows

Cobwebs in the Windows *by Shirley Hughes*

Fabric needed for a lap quilt

White: 1½ yards
Blue: 1½ yards
Flower: ¾ yard
Border and binding: 1½ yards

Cutting instructions

12 Attic Windows (see p. 30)

White: cut 3 x 3½" strips, cut into 12 x 10" lengths
Blue: cut 3 x 3½" strips, cut into 12 x 10" lengths
Flower: cut twelve 6½" squares

12 Mitred Squares (see p.25)

White: cut 14 x 1⅝" strips
Blue: cut 14 x 1⅝" strips

Border

Cut 6 x 4½" strips

12 Attic Window blocks
12 Mitred Square blocks
Make 7 strip sets using alternating white and blue 1⅝" strips.

Stitch alternating attic window and mitred square blocks together into quilt top.

Shirley made her quilt top into a quillow using the traditional method. She used a cotton wadding and hand quilted.

What if...

...you appliquéd spiders in some of the windows?

...you used a fabric with a view in each window?

...a photograph printed onto fabric was placed in each window?

...a graduated fabric was used in the mitred square? (See Teresa's quilt on p. 1.)

Fabric needed for lap quilt

Light: 1¾ yards

Dark: 1¾ yards

Red: 1 yard, includes binding

Border: ¾ yard

Cutting Instructions

12 Quarter square triangles (see p. 44)

Light: cut 2 x 10¼" strips

Dark: cut 2 x 10¼" strips

12 Mitred Squares (see p. 25)

Light: cut 16 x 1⅝" strips

Dark: cut 18 x 1⅝" strips

Red: cut one 1⅝" strip

Borders

Red: cut 6 x 1" strips for borders

Blue: cut 6 x 3½" strips

Oriental Treasures *by Jan Allen*

12 Quarter square triangles

1 Cut 2 x 10¼" strips in 6 light and 6 dark squares and use to sew 12 quarter square triangle blocks.

12 Mitred Squares

2 Use 16 x 1⅝" strips in light and dark to sew 8 strip sets each using light/ dark/ light/ dark strips. Sew 11 mitred square blocks.

3 Stitch one mitred square block using 1⅝" strips in red, dark, light and dark.

4 Stitch alternating blocks together as shown.

Border

5 Stitch 1" red border to 3½" blue border, stitch to quilt sides and mitre.

6 Bind in red fabric

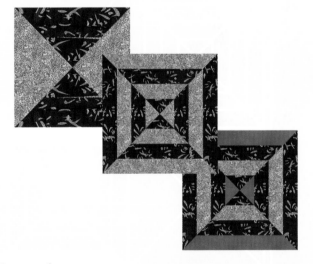

Jan made a wrap-around pillow to give an extra oriental feel to her magic pillow. She used an 80/20 cotton/polyester wadding and quilted with a navy big stitch.

Stars in the Cabin

Stars in the Cabin *by Heather Langdon.*

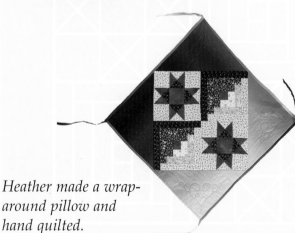

Heather made a wrap-around pillow and hand quilted.

Fabric needed for lap quilt

1st light print (L1): ¾ yard

2nd light print (L2): ½ yard

3rd light print (light blue – L3): ¾ yard

Red: ¾ yard

1st and 2nd dark prints (D1 and D2): ½ yard of each

Darkest print (D3): ¾ yard

Border blue: 1 yard

Cutting instructions

12 Log Cabin blocks (see p. 20)

Light: cut 1¾" wide strips (2 L1, 3 L2, 5 L3)

Dark: cut 1¾" wide strips (3 D1, 4 D2, 5 D3)

Red: cut one 2" wide strip

12 Star blocks (see p. 39)

Red: cut one 3½" strip, cut into 12 squares; cut 2 x 4¼" strips, cut into 24 squares

1st light (L1): cut 2 x 3½" strips, and cut into 24 squares; then cut one 4¼" strip, and cut into 6 squares.

3rd light (L3): cut 2 x 3½" strips, and cut into 24 squares; then cut one 4¼" strip, and cut into 6 squares.

Darkest print (D3): cut 2 x 4¼" strips, cut into 12 squares

Border

Cut 6 x 4½" strips

12 Log Cabin Squares

1 Stitch two light and then two dark logs around the centre square. Repeat to make three rounds, creating a block with a strong diagonal.

12 Star blocks

2 Six of these use the palest light fabric (L1) and six use the darkest light fabric (L3). The stars are created using four quarter square triangle units, made from three different fabrics: red, the darkest print (D3) and either L1 or L3.

3 Make 24 quarter square units using the 4¼″ squares in lightest print (L1), darkest print (D3) and red.

4 Draw a diagonal line on the wrong side of each light (L1) square.

5 Place 6 red squares right sides together with the light squares

6 Stitch a scant ¼″ seam either side of the drawn line, press. Cut on drawn line and press to dark.

7 Repeat with remaining 6 red squares right sides to 6 dark (D3) squares.

8 Take a light/red square and a dark/red square, place right sides together so that the reds are not opposite one another.

9 Draw a diagonal line on wrong side of square.

10 Stitch a scant ¼″ seam either side of the drawn line, press.

11 Cut apart, press to red. You should now have 24 quarter square triangles

13 Sew units into rows alternating quarter square triangles with a light 3½″ square or nine patch.

14 Stitch 3 rows into a block

15 Make 6 blocks. Repeat with the darkest of the light fabrics (L3) and the remaining red and darkest (D3) squares.

16 Stitch alternating log cabin and star blocks into quilt top. Add 4½″ border.

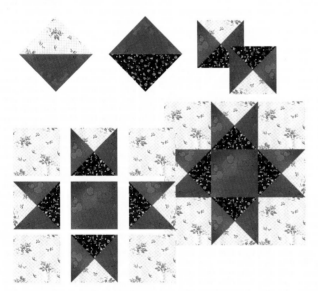

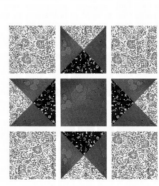

Celtic Stars

Celtic Stars, *pieced by Susan Prior and machine quilted by Jan Chandler.*

Fabric needed for lap quilt

Light: 1¾ yards

Red: 1½ yards, includes border

Print: 1½ yards, includes binding

Turquoise: ¼ yard

Cutting instructions

12 Chain blocks (see p. 39)

Light: 4 x 3½" strips, cut into 48 squares; plus 4 x 2" strips

Print: cut 5 x 2" strips

Turquoise: cut one 2" strip

12 Star blocks (see p. 39)

Light: cut 4 x 3½" strips, cut into 48 squares; 2 x 4¼" strips, cut into 12 squares; and 3 x 1½" strips.

Turquoise: cut 3 x 1½" strips

Print: cut 2 x 4¼" strips, cut into 12 squares

Red: cut 3 x 4¼" strips, cut into 24 squares

Border

Red: cut 6 x 4½" strips

12 Chain blocks

1 Layer one turquoise and one print 2" strip right sides together, make into 12 x 3½" four-patch units.

2 Layer 4 light and 4 print 2" strips, in pairs, right sides together. Stitch into 48 x 3½" four patch units.

3 Sew units into rows, alternating four patch with a light 3½" square.

4 Stitch 3 rows into a block; make 12 blocks.

12 Star blocks

12 Nine patch centres (see p. 32)

5 Use 1½″ strips in light and dark fabrics to sew the two strip sets.

6 Cut 1½″ pieces from each strip set and sew together to make the nine patch 3½″ centre unit.

Quarter square triangle units (see p. 44)

7 Each star block has four quarter square triangle units, made from three different fabrics.

8 Make 48 quarter square units. Use the 4¼″ squares in light, print and red.

9 Draw a diagonal line on the wrong side of each print square.

10 Place 12 red squares right sides together with the 12 print squares.

11 Stitch a scant ¼″ seam either side of the drawn line, press.

12 Cut on drawn line and press to red. Repeat with remaining 12 red squares right sides to 12 light squares.

13 Take a light/red square and a print/red square and place right sides together, reversing darks.

14 Draw a diagonal line on wrong side of square.

15 Stitch a scant ¼″ seam either side of the drawn line, press. Cut apart, press to reds.

16 You should now have 48 quarter square triangles. Check each measures 3½″.

17 Sew units into rows alternating quarter square triangles with a light 3½″ square or nine patch.

18 Stitch 3 rows into a block; make 12 blocks.

19 Alternating 12 chain blocks and 12 star blocks, stitch into a quilt top.

20 Add a 4¼″ border.

Left: Detail of Celtic Stars, *showing the machine quilting done by Jan Chandler on a long arm machine.*

Right: Susan made a slip-in pillow. The quilt has an 80/20 cotton/ polyester wadding. The pillow has a cotton wadding and was hand quilted by Susan.

71

Quilt top construction

Tidy the blocks before joining: trim excess threads and press well, checking that each block is square and the correct size. The 9½" Omnigrid square is ideal for trimming blocks to the correct size.

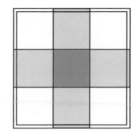
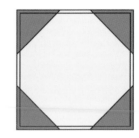

Twenty four blocks are needed for the lap quilt, and twelve for the mini quilt.

Blocks into rows – lap quilt

1   Arrange 9½" blocks in rows of four; stitch together.

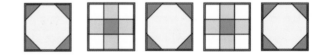

2   Set out all six rows.

3   You can press the intersecting seams so that alternate rows have the seams pressed in the same direction, which opposes the adjoining rows. This helps the 'nestling and wrestling' (see p.14) when matching seams. However, I prefer to twist the seams as I stitch, so as to get all my seams to oppose.

4   Press the new horizontal seams open to help distribute bulk.

5   Press the top well before adding borders. Check that all four corners are square, and trim if necessary.

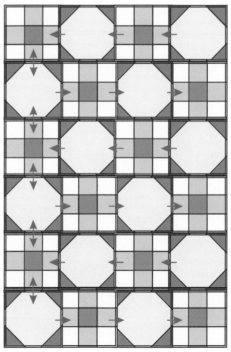

Cut 4½″ wide strips from one fabric for borders, or make a simple patched border.

Lap quilt

The side strips need to be 54½″ (6 blocks x 9 = 54½″) long. Check this measurement against your quilt top. You may need to piece the side strips from two fabric strips to make the 54½″ length.

I always pre-cut both side strips to the same length, and then make the quilt top fit the pre-cut strips. Decide if you prefer to have the joining seams opposite one another on the quilt top or staggered.

Pin (matching the corners first, then half way), and ease the quilt top in to fit the strips. This way you are unlikely to end up with one side longer than the other. Press the seams out towards the border.

Measure the quilt top and bottom. Cut two strips using the correct measurement (44½″) and attach as before. Press away from the centre.

Mini quilt

Cut 3½″ wide border strips. The side strips should be 36½″ (4 blocks x 9 = 36½) long, and the top and bottom strips 33½″ long.

Attach the borders following the instructions for the lap quilt above.

Mitred borders

You may choose to have mitred corners in the quilt borders. Patchwork patterns that use diagonal seams may look better if the corner seams are also on the diagonal.

Mitres look very clever, but are easy if they are made using a similar technique to Attic Windows. The cut border strips are longer than the quilt, as the excess fabric is needed for the mitre.

Lap quilt

Cut 4½" wide strips from one fabric for quilt border.

Two side strips, 68" long.

Two strips for top and bottom, 58" long.

Mini quilt

Cut 3½" wide strips from one fabric for quilt border.

Two side strips 49" long.

Two strips for top and bottom 48" long.

1 Fold quilt sides and borders in half, and mark with a pin.

2 Matching halfway points and right sides together, pin and stitch borders to quilt. Begin and end stitching one stitch less than ¼" from corners. Backstitch to reinforce.

3 Press seams out towards the border.

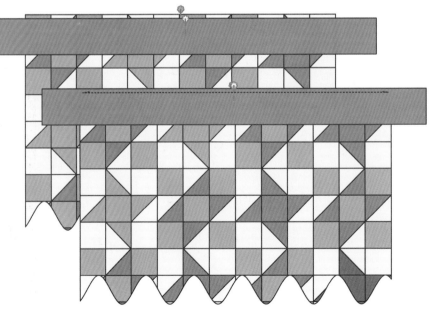

4 Arrange the first corner to be mitred on the ironing board, right side up, with the border strips at the top and right side. You may need to pin the quilt to the ironing board to prevent it from falling off or pulling the corner. Left handers may wish to mirror image this.

5 At the corner fold the excess side strip under to lie in line with the top strip, forming the mitre. Check the mitre with the 45° line on a ruler. Place the pre-heated iron carefully on the 'mitre' and hold for five seconds (in the time it takes to slowly say 'got you'), This pressed mark will be your sewing line. Place a pin near the mitre.

6 Carefully turn the patchwork to the wrong side and move the pin to the reverse side without disturbing the mitre. Add more pins to hold the mitre in place. Stitch on the pressed line, starting at the outside corner and stitching to within one stitch of the inside corner. Reverse stitch to anchor the threads.

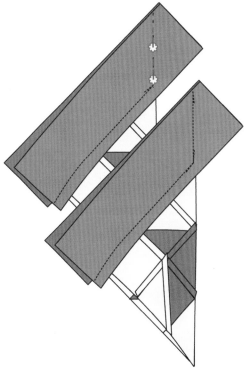

7 Check the seam from the right side. It should lie flat with a mitred corner. Trim the seam to ¼". Press the seam open.

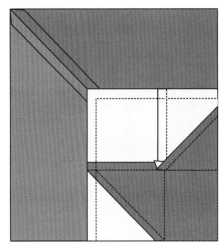

8 Repeat on remaining three corners.

Borders with fancy corners

An alternative way of finishing the quilt is to create a small block or part block for each corner. This, like the mitred corner, gives a nice symmetrical feel to the quilt and is quick and easy to do. The easiest fancy corner is simply a 4½" square.

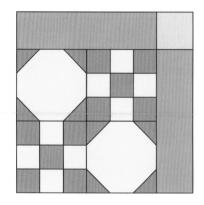

1 Cut the side borders as on p.73 and sew on. Cut the top and bottom borders the width of your quilt top and sew on the four contrasting squares before sewing the border to the quilt top.

2 For fancy corners for the magic 9-patch, just cut up one more block to give the corners you need.

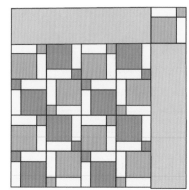

3 For other blocks you may need to create a special unit for your corners.

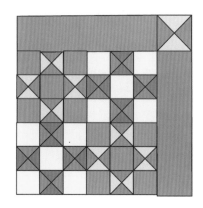

QH Tip

Many of the quilts in this book incorporate a narrow strip between the border and the main top. This provides a neat frame to the top, and is produced by taking a strip of fabric 1½" wide and ironing it in half to give a ¾" strip. Cut to the length and width of the top, and position with the folded side away from the edge between the top and the border before stitching on the latter.

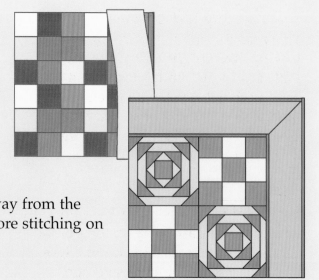

Quilt layering

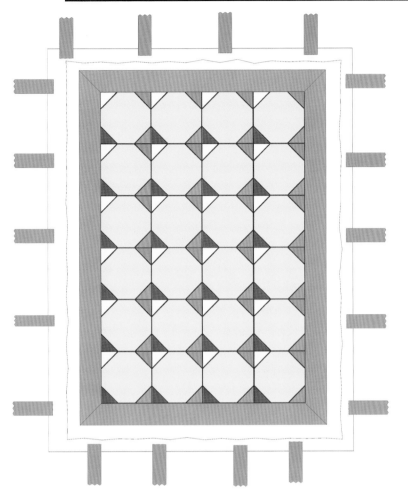

Traditionally a quilt top is layered with wadding and backing before quilting and binding. This stage is not needed if you are following my method of Quillow construction.

1 Place the backing wrong side up, on a clean large table. Use masking tape to anchor the backing to the table, stretching the backing but taking care not to pull it out of shape. The backing can be pinned to a carpeted floor using strong quilt pins, stabbed at an angle into the carpet.

2 Place the wadding on top, smoothing it over the backing.

3 Place the pressed and tidied quilt top (no stray threads) right side up on the wadding. Centre the top, making sure the quilt is parallel to the edges of the backing.

4 The layers need to be tacked temporarily before tying or quilting.

Tacking/basting methods

Use one of these methods to keep the quilt layers together:

a **Hand tacking** Tack by hand using a long straw needle and a light coloured tacking thread. Cut a very long thread and start in the centre tacking out to the edge with half the length. Pick up the other half of the thread and tack from the centre out to the opposite edge. Tack a grid of 6″ parallel lines over the whole quilt.

b **Safety pins** Use rustproof 1″ safety pins spaced 3–4″ apart. Start pinning in the centre and work towards outer edges, smoothing quilt top out as you go.

c **The Quilt Tack System** This is my favourite method as it is relatively quick and painless. It can be used when preparing for any of the quilting methods. A gun is used to 'shoot' small plastic tacks through the quilt layers. I always use a plastic grid placed between the table and backing to protect the needle and work surface from damage.

d **Spray glue** Recently several spray glues have been developed especially for quilters. They provide a temporary stick to the layers without gumming up needles when quilting. The adhesive is very light. Follow the instructions provided by the manufacturer.

Quillow Pillow

A quillow needs a pillow to hide the quilt! The pillow front is made up and quilted separately before attaching to the quilt, to form a pocket. It is this space between the pillow and the quilt that becomes the secret pocket for hiding the quilt.

Lap Pillow front

Sew together four 9″ blocks in any combination to make an 18½″ square.

Add 2½″ border strips to all four sides to increase the pillow size to 22½″ .

The pillow will be reduced by approximately 1″ once the quillow construction is complete to give a 21″ finished size.

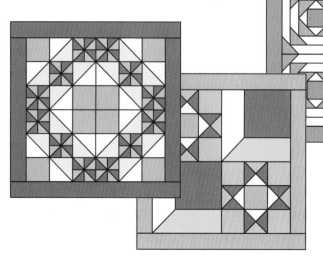

QH Tip

If the pillow front has a directional pattern (e.g. Attic Windows) be sure to leave the side at the *top* of the design open.

Mini pillow front

Sew a 9″ block, add 2½″ border strips to all four sides to bring the pillow size up to 13½″.

The pillow will be reduced by approximately 1″ once quillow construction is complete to give a 12″ finished size.

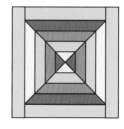

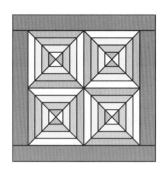

Assembling the quillow pillow

1. The pillow back is cut from fabric identical to the quilt back, so that you will not notice it once it is attached. Cut a piece that matches the pillow front exactly.

2. Cut wadding slightly larger than pillow front. I prefer to use a 100% cotton wadding as it handles easily and can be ironed.

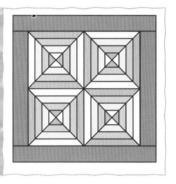

3. Lay the wadding flat on your work surface. Place pillow front right sides up on wadding.

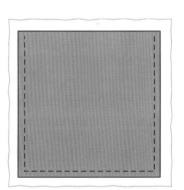

4. Lay pillow back right side down on pillow front, matching raw edges. Pin, leaving one side open. Tack if necessary.

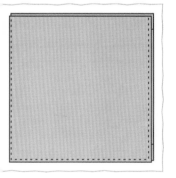

5. Stitch around all three sides using a ¼" seam.

6. Trim wadding close to stitching to remove extra bulk. Trim corners.

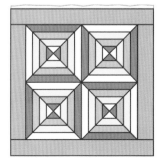

7. Turn pillow right sides out, through the opening.

8. Tie or quilt. Leave the opening *open*.

Slip-in Pillow

The quilt can be folded and inserted into a pillow slip when not in use. The quilt forms the padding of the pillow, but the pillow is not attached to the quilt!

Lap Pillow front

1 Sew together four blocks in any combination to make an 18½" square.

2 Add 2½" border strips all round to increase the size to 22½".

3 Cut a 23" square each of wadding and backing fabric. The backing fabric forms a lining inside the pillow.

4 Make a sandwich of three layers – backing wrong side up, wadding in between, and pillow front right side up on top – just as you would in a quilt.

5 Quilt or tie the layers.

6 Trim the backing and wadding to fit the pillow top, making sure corners are square.

Reverse side of pillow slip

1 This is made from two pieces of fabric which will overlap to form an opening for the folded quilt. Cut one piece of fabric 22½" x 23", and a second piece 22½" x 28". Fold each piece in half – 22½" x 11½, 22½" x 14". Press. Stitch ¼" from folded edge to keep this edge folded.

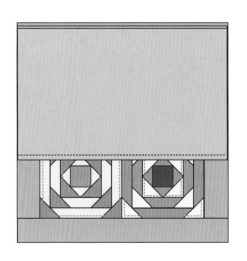

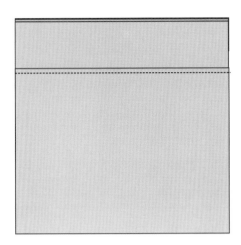

2 Place smaller backing section right sides together on pillow front. Place larger section right side down on remaining pillow front.

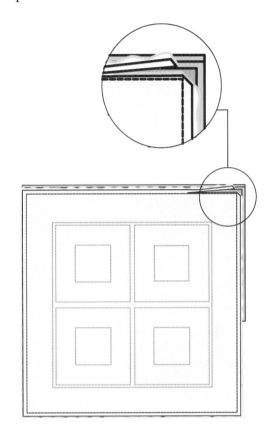

3 Pin, stitch around all four sides with a ¼″ seam. Trim corners, trim wadding and fabric on patchwork side to ⅛″ (this will help you to roll the seam to the edge). Turn pillow through to right side. From the outside press the pillow edge neatly so that the seam is on the edge.

4 Stitch in the ditch between the patchwork and border to form a square in which the quilt can be folded to become the pillow padding. The pillow is now ready for its quilt insert.

QH Tips

Use a cotton wadding, as it helps to be able to iron it later.

To give a slightly larger pocket for your quilt you may prefer to use two borders instead of one, and sew between these two rather than between the block and the border.

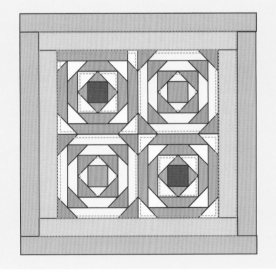

Mini pillow front

1 Take a block, and add two 2½" borders to bring the pillow size up to 17½".

2 Cut an 18" square each of wadding and backing fabric. The backing fabric forms a lining inside the pillow.

3 Make a sandwich of three layers (backing wrong side up, wadding in between, and pillow right side up on top – just as you would in a quilt). Quilt or tie the layers. Trim the backing and wadding to fit the pillow top, making sure corners are square.

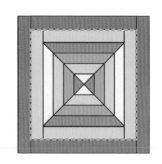

Reverse side of pillow slip

This is made from two pieces of fabric which will overlap to form an opening for the folded quilt.

1 Cut one piece of fabric 17½"x 20", and a second piece 17½"x 24". Fold each piece in half (17½"x 10" and 17½"x 12"). Press. Stitch ¼" from folded edge to keep this edge folded. Place smaller backing section right sides together on pillow front.

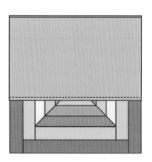

2 Place larger section right side down on remaining pillow front. Pin, stitch around all four sides with a ¼" seam. Trim corners and turn through.

3 Pin, stitch around all four sides with a ¼" seam. Trim corners, trim wadding and fabric on patchwork side to ⅛" (this will help you to roll the seam to the edge). Turn pillow through to right side.

4 From the outside press the pillow edge neatly so that the seam is on the very edge. Stitch in the ditch between the two borders to form a square in which the quilt can be folded to become the pillow padding. The pillow is now ready for its quilt insert.

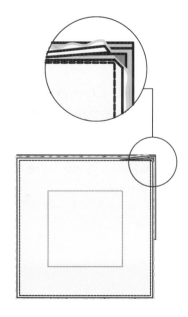

Pillow closure

To prevent the pillow gaping open, use one of the methods shown here.

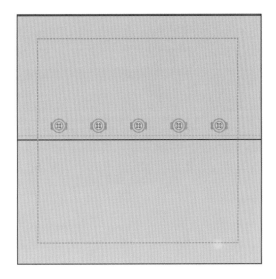

Buttons and buttonholes

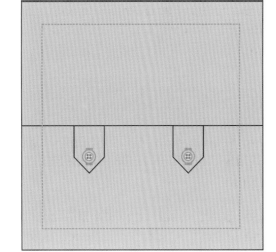

Tabs with buttons and Velcro dots

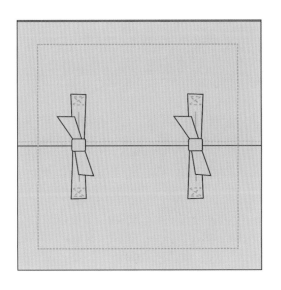

Ribbons or ties

QH Tip

Sew any ties, tabs, velcro or buttons etc. on to your back panels before attaching them to your pillow front.

This would also be a good time to sew on any labels!

Wrapped Pillow

Rosemary Muntus first showed me one of these pillows. She had made it in a quilted Sashiko style and tied it round a pillow pad. My imagination took it a few steps further, first as a wrap cover to enclose a quilt and then as a patchwork square (an alternative to the Sashiko quilting). Measurements are given for enclosing either a lap or mini size quilts.

Lap pillow

1 Stitch together four 9½" blocks. Press. Block now measures 18½".

2 Cut two 14" fabric squares, cut each in half diagonally. Each triangle is stitched to one side of the block.

3 Right sides together, stitch the longest bias triangle side to the block edge, taking care not to stretch the fabric. Carefully, press away from centre. Trim square ¼" from each inside corner to make a square approximately 26".

4 Layer with wadding and backing, and tie or quilt.

Binding/Ties

1 Cut two 2" x 26" fabric strips, and two 2" x 46" fabric strips.

2 Stitch short binding strips to opposite sides of the quilted square. Place strips right side down on the front of the square. Starting at the corner, stitch using ½" seam. Stop at the corner. Fold edges in and slip stitch to back. The longer strips are placed on remaining opposite sides and have 10" hanging

QH Tip

Fold block in half and mark crease with a pin. Carefully find the centre of the bias triangle side and mark with a pin. Matching pins helps you to correctly position the triangle to the block.

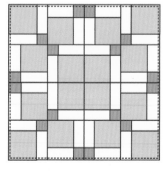

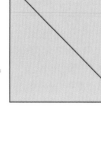

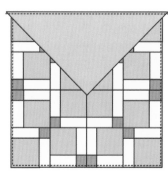

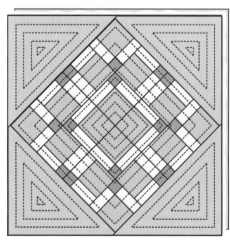

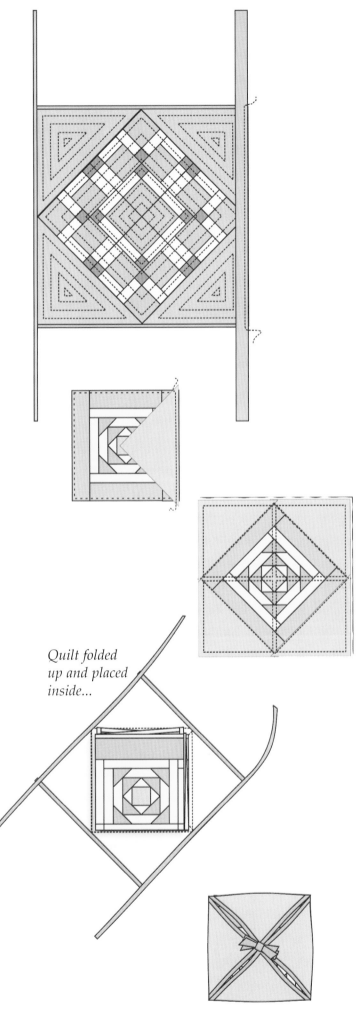

Quilt folded up and placed inside...

loose from each corner. These become the ties. Sew as before. Stitch from one corner to the next corner, leave the remainder of the strip hanging.

3 Slip stitch binding to back of square as before.

4 To complete the ties, press along the centre. Tuck raw edges in and slip stitch or machine together.

Mini

1 Take a block, add a 1½" wide strip border to all four sides, and press away from centre. Block now measures 11½".

2 Cut two 9" fabric squares, and cut each in half diagonally. Each triangle is stitched to one side of the block.

3 Right sides together, stitch the longest bias triangle side to the block edge. Press away from centre. Trim to make a square approximately 16".

4 Layer with wadding and backing, tie or quilt. Tack outside edges from edge.

Binding/Ties

Cut two 2" x 16" fabric strips, and two 2" x 36" fabric strips.

Stitch short binding strips to opposite sides of the quilted square. Place strips right side down on the front of the square. Starting at the corner, stitch using ½" seam. Stop at the corner. Fold edges in and slip stitch to back. The longer strips are placed on remaining opposite sides and have 10" hanging loose from each corner. These become the ties. Sew as before. Stitch from one corner to the next corner, leave the remainder of the strip hanging.

Slip stitch binding to back of square as before. To complete the ties, press along the centre. Tuck raw edges in and slip stitch or machine together.

Quillow assembly using binding

Advantages

- If you have made a quilt before then this method will seem familiar to you as you quilt the layers first (see p.76) and attach the binding before completely attaching the pillow.

- Ideal for those who want the quilting pattern to continue over the whole quilt, as you can quilt without a pillow getting in the way.

1 Find the centre point along the open side of a finished quillow pillow (see pp. 78–79), and mark with a pin.

2 Lay out the quilted quilt. Find the centre of the top short side and mark with a pin.

3 Place the right side of the pillow (the patchwork side) face down on the reverse side of the quilt; match pins on pillow with pins on quilt. Lay on a flat surface. Pin and tack the top raw edges together ready for binding.

Disadvantages

- It takes longer to make the quillow because you are adding a binding.

- The pillow attachment is weaker.

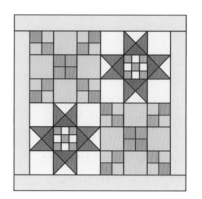

4 Pin the pillow in place on the back of the quilt and hand stitch into place down the two sides. *Leave the bottom side open.*

5 Bind the edges of the quilt using your favourite binding method or my favourite which is the double fold binding on page 92. The binding measurements are a little wider than usual, as it has to incorporate the extra bulk of the pillow edge at the top of the quilt.

QH Tip

It's important to sew the pillow securely in place with strong thread; use either quilting thread, doubled, or button thread. I like to stitch both sides twice and add extra stitches at the bottom corners to reinforce. Take care that you do not stitch right through to the other side, which would spoil the front of your quilt. And leave the bottom edge open so that you can pull the pillow front through when you need to hide your quilt.

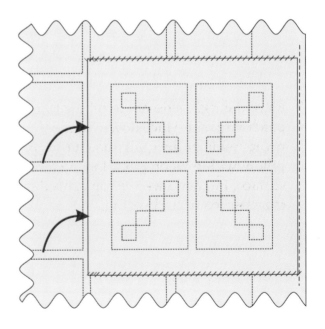

'No binding' quillow assembly

- It requires no binding, and is therefore a quicker method.

Disadvantages

- As the tying/quilting is the final stage, the pillow is already in place and can get in the way, particularly if machine quilting.

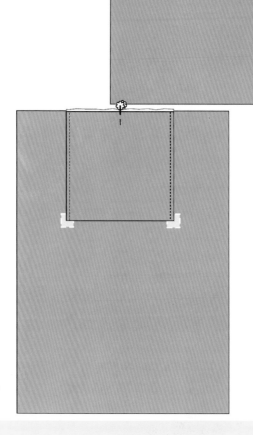

1 Find the centre point along the open side of the pillow of the pillow front, mark with a pin.

2 Prepare the quilt backing by matching it to the quilt top. Trim one to fit the other so that both have raw edges matching all round. Take the quilt backing only, find the centre of the top short side, and mark with a pin.

3 Right sides together, match pins on pillow with pins on quilt backing.

4 Cut two 2" squares of fabric (either the same as the backing or a calico). Fold squares in half and pin under the bottom corners of the pillow, on the reverse of the backing fabric. This will help to strengthen the corners, which can be stressed when the pillow is turned in and out.

5 Starting at the outside edge, top stitch down each side of the pillow through all the layers. Reverse stitch at each end.

QH Tips

If you have a walking foot for your machine, use it when sewing quilt layers together to prevent shifting between the layers.

I like to finish my stitching at the bottom pillow corners by using a quarter-inch length of satin stitch, rather like the reinforcement stitching that you see on jeans pockets.

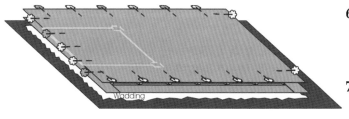

Wadding

6 Place the quilt wadding on a flat surface. Place quilt *top* right side up on wadding.

7 Place fabric backing (including the pillow) *right side down* on the quilt top. Pin at right angles to fabric edge, ensuring that the raw edges match. Pin all around the quilt, leaving an 18" gap in the middle of the bottom edge.

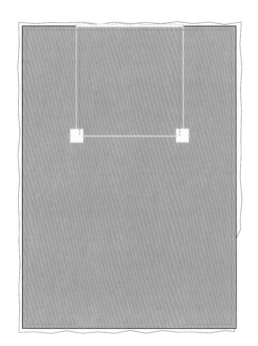

8 Stitch all round the edge, except the gap. Check that all the layers have been caught in the stitching. I usually increase my seam allowance by ½" to catch the layers. Trim wadding back, almost to stitching, to reduce bulk.

9 Turn right side out through the opening and admire your work!

10 Roll the quilt edges between your finger and thumb to help the seam to the edge, and safety pin in place. Add more safety pins to the quilt centre to keep the layers temporarily in place (but avoid pillow).

11 Turn in opening raw edges and press fabric only, not the wadding! Hand sew to close the opening, or use the blind hem foot on your machine to stitch as close as you can to the edge.

12 Tie or quilt.

13 Remove the safety pins!

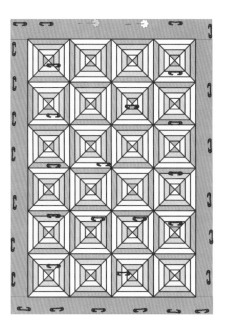

QH Tip

Place a piece of cardboard in the pillow pocket to prevent the pillow from being tied to the quilt.

Folding a quillow

1 Lay the quilt out, right
side up.

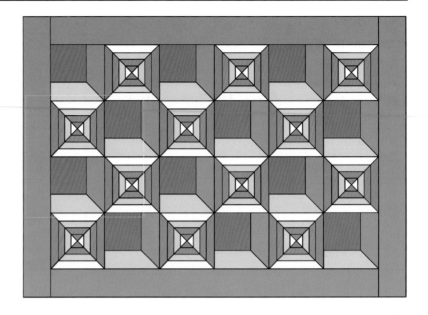

2 Fold in the sides to
within the pillow edge.

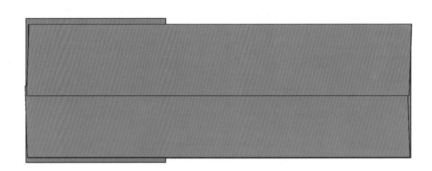

3 Turn the pillow right
sides out. Fold the quilt
end to the pillow and
then fold again to tuck
inside the pillow.

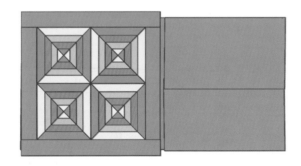

4 Hold the pillow at the
open end and gently
shake to let the quilt
settle into its magic
hiding place.

The quilt layers need to be tied or quilted to keep them together. You may prefer to hand or machine quilt. Or try the quick tying stitches which have been used on quilts in 'Magic Pillows, Hidden Quilts' which, like the patchwork, are quick to do. After all you want to start using the quilt!

Embroidery threads are used for tying. Large needles are needed - chenille, milliners and 3″ doll needles. The longer needles are ideal for travelling the distance in the wadding, a requirement of some of the stitches. Stitches are spaced 3–4″ apart when using polyester and wool waddings, 6–8″ apart when cotton wadding is used.

Beginning your Stitching

No knot method: use a thread twice as long as you consider comfortable. Start your stitch by pulling through half the thread only, and stitch until this is used. Later go back and thread up this excess length and continue your stitching.

Or: backstitch once or twice on the edge of the quilt; it will be covered later by the binding.

Ending your Stitching

Take a tiny backstitch on top of the last stitch, splitting the thread as you return to the surface. Insert the needle into the wadding very near to where the thread exited and travel for approximately 2″, do not go through to backing. Return to the quilt top, hold the thread taut and clip it close to the surface of the quilt. The thread end will be trapped in the quilt layers.

Big Stitch

Sew a quilting / running stitch with big stitches ¼″ long. Keep the stitches even in length. Follow a marked quilting pattern or sew **free hand** without marking the quilt top.

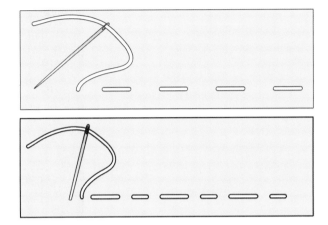

Cross Stitch

Start at A and take a stitch through all the layers at B, coming up at C. Insert the needle at D and travel through the wadding only to the starting point of the next stitch.

Crow Footing

Start at A. Hold the thread down with your thumb and insert the needle at B. Go through all the layers bringing the needle out at C. Pull up the thread to form a V shape, then insert the needle at D, on the opposite side of the thread from C. Travel through the wadding only to the starting point of the next stitch.

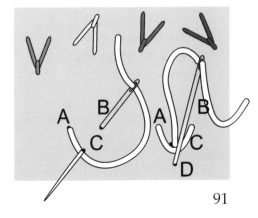

91

Binding

1 Tack through all the layers ⅛″ from the edge, to hold them all together.

2 Cut 2½″ strips from your chosen binding fabric, on the lengthways or crosswise grain. I prefer to use the lengthways grain, as it has little stretch.

3 Join the binding strips together by placing them perpendicular to one another, end to end, with right sides together. Mark a diagonal line and stitch on the line. Cut away the excess ¼″ outside the stitching and press seams open. Join the strips until you have a length equal to the quilt perimeter plus 18″. (For a lap quilt the perimeter will be 230″; for a mini-quilt, 168″).

4 Cut the beginning of the binding at a 45-degree angle. Turn in the edge ¼″ and press.

5 Fold the binding strip in half lengthways, wrong sides together, and press.

6 Place the binding on the right side of the quilt, aligning raw edges of the binding and the quilt. My starting point is on the bottom quilt edge, approximately 6″ away from a corner.

7 Using a walking foot, begin sewing 2″ from the strip end, and, stopping ¼″ from the first quilt corner, backstitch.

8 Remove the quilt from the machine and cut the threads.

9 Fold the binding up, then back down so that the fold is even with the quilt edge. Pin.

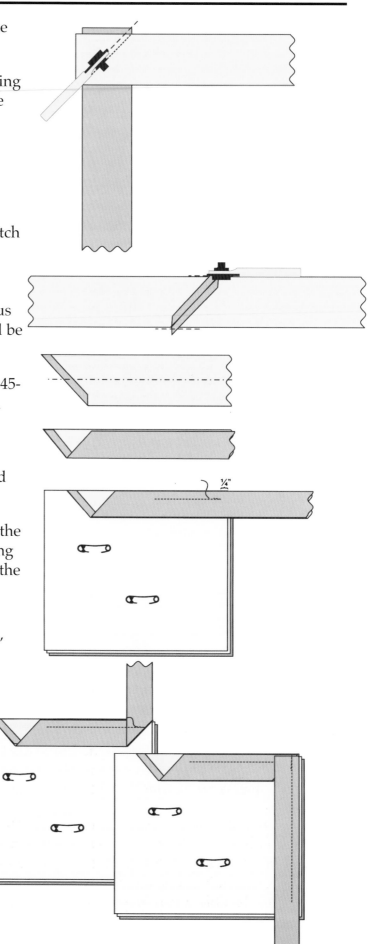

10 Begin stitching at the edge of the next side, backstitching to secure the threads. Continue sewing to the next corner. Repeat at all four corners.

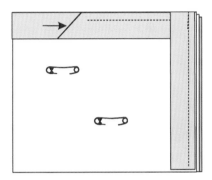

11 As you near the start point, cut the binding strip and tuck the end into the folded strip. Finish the sewing and backstitch.

12 Blindstitch the folded edge to the tucked strip.

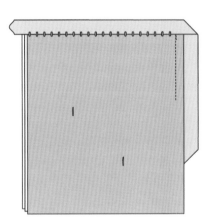

13 Turn the binding to the back of the quilt, and blindstitch to the backing, covering the previous stitching. Fold the corners as shown.

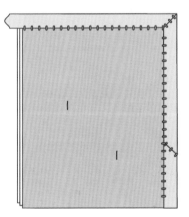

Caring for your quilt

Lap quilts and mini quilts are designed to be well used, and will need to be washed more often than other heirloom quilts.

Their size makes it easy to place them in a washing machine (on the gentlest wash, with the mildest washing liquid you can find). A short spin is needed to remove the excess water. Tumble dry, or dry the quilt flat. If you are giving the quilt away, simple washing instructions attached to the quilt will be appreciated.

The quilts are meant to be stored in their magic pillows, so don't worry if they look a little creased when you unfold them. Once they are in use the creases soon disappear!

Larger quilts

'I love the patterns but want a larger quilt!'

Several people said that to me in the course of writing this book; and I'm happy to say that the answer is very simple.

To make a larger quilt, you simply need to make more blocks – and as all the patterns are based on 9" patchwork blocks it is easy to design your own unique quilt in the size you want. Additional borders can also be used. Suggested measurements are given for single and double quilts.

Single bed size (54" x 81")

Width 5 x 9" blocks

Length 8 x 9" blocks

Make 40 blocks in all

Border 4½"

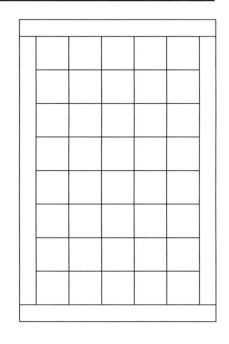

Double bed size (90" x 90")

Width 8 x 9" blocks

Length 8 x 9" blocks

Make 64 blocks in all

Two 4½" borders are used

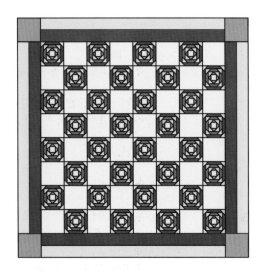

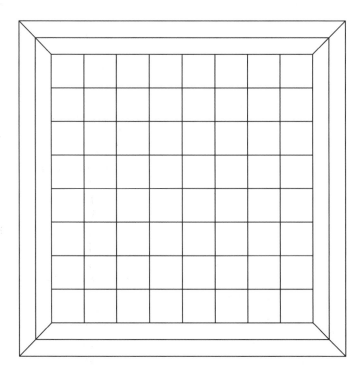

Index

Page numbers in italic refer to pictures only, while those in bold refer to important sections.

Addresses

Oakcraft

Distributors for RJR, Fabri-Quilt & Av-Lyn Creations

14 Thurrock Commercial Centre,
Juliette Way,
Purfleet, Essex RM15 4YG

Tel. +44 (0)1708 680789

E-mail: sales@oakcraft.com

Timeless Treasures (Europe) Ltd

Unit 3, Halifax House,
Coronation Road, High Wycombe,
Buckinghamshire, HP12 3SE

Tel. +44 (0)1494 514088

Custom machine quilting

Quilting Solutions
Firethorn, Rattlesden Road,
Drinkstone,
Bury St Edmunds,
Suffolk IP30 9TL

Tel: +44 (0)1449 736280

Web: www.quiltingsolutions.co.uk

Design and layout

Creative Computing
Rosemary Muntus and Allan Scott
Old Mill House, The Causeway,
Hitcham, Suffolk IP7 7NF, UK

Tel: +44 (0)1449 741747

E-mail: creatively42@aol.com

Web: www.thecraftycomputer.co.uk

Designs from *Electric Quilt*

Electric Quilt Company
419 Gould Street, Suite 2
Bowling Green
OH 43402
USA

Tel: +1 419 352 1134

Web: www.wcnet.org/ElectricQuiltCo/

Distribution outside the UK

Quilters' Resource Inc
PO Box 148850
Chicago
Illinois 60614
USA

Tel: 312-278-5795

About the author

Karin Hellaby was born in the north-east of England of Norwegian parents: her first language was Norwegian. She studied for a Home Economics teaching degree from the University of Wales. Now she lives in Suffolk, and is the single parent of three wonderful boys.

Karin started teaching quiltmaking around her kitchen table when pregnant with her third son, Alexander, who is now 12 years old. Quilters Haven opened in 1993 as a teaching centre, with a shop alongside to supply the students, a unique concept in England at that time. It moved to its 17th-century timber-framed building in 1996. The attractive shop, with gallery room and teaching area, attracts quiltmakers and teachers from all over the world. In 1998 Karin, with the help of her son Ross (then aged 15), won the Kile Scholarship – International Retailer of the Year. The next step was to write a book. That was *Sew a Row Quilts* – and this book came next!